"Real writing is re-writing. Paul Chitlik provides practical, positive advice, not for screenwriters alone but for playwrights, novelists, and all scribes struggling to do the best work that they can."
    — Prof. Richard Walter,
        UCLA Screenwriting Chairman

"Paul Chitlik is an inspired teacher and a master of writing craftsmanship. His book will help lift your script to the next level and make it stand out from the crowd. You can't afford *not* to listen to his practical and pithy advice. Great writing is smart rewriting. This book shows you how."
    — Laurie Hutzler, Film and Television Writer,
        Visiting Associate Professor of Screenwriting at UCLA
        and Author, *One Hour Screenwriter* and *The Character Map*

"I've used Paul's method on several of my scripts, and it really works. When it comes to rewriting, he's the master."
    — Dean Alioto, Writer/Director, *LA Dicks*

"With this book, Paul Chitlik offers a concise and highly accessible guide to the craft of rewriting. Beginning and established screenwriters alike will benefit from Paul's insights and experience in the trenches. I recommend it highly."
    — Ernie Contreras, Screenwriter, *Fairy Tale: A True Story*

"This book breaks down not only rewriting, but screenwriting in general, to its smallest possible components, allowing the writer to examine his story piece-by-piece and reassemble it as a stronger whole. It's filled with valuable exercises to inspire the writer to keep thinking about his story and push on to the next level."
    — Bobby Moresco,
        Academy Award®-winning Screenwriter, *Crash*

"*Rewrite* is the most important step in getting the audience's emotional investment on the screen. Emotional architecture is what it's *all* about."
— Quinn K. Redeker,
Oscar® Nomination for Co-writing *The Deer Hunter*

"The ability to rewrite effectively is the most important skill a working screenwriter can possess. I use Paul's method on every project. It is the single best way to pinpoint a script's problems and figure out how to fix them."
— Dan Mazeau, Screenwriter, *Land of Lost Things*

"*Rewrite* really helps you understand the difference between the first draft and the final (shootable) draft, and how to get from point A to point B. I highly recommend *Rewrite* as a practical guide for all screenwriters and directors."
— David Hurd, Editor, *www.p3update.com*

"Paul Chitlik makes rewriting look easy by re-inventing the writing process, and that's a testament to his excellence as a teacher."
— Steve Duncan, Associate Professor and Chair,
Screenwriting Department, Loyola Marymount
University School of Film & Television

"Paul Chitlik does an amazing job of dissecting the hardest job facing any writer: the dreaded re-write. Step-by-step, word-by-word, he is like a writing coach looking over your shoulder. Excellent book."
— Matthew Terry, *www.hollywoodlitsales.com*

rewrite

A STEP-BY-STEP GUIDE TO STRENGTHEN STRUCTURE, CHARACTERS, AND DRAMA IN YOUR SCREENPLAY

paul chitlik

Published by Michael Wiese Productions
12400 Ventura Blvd, # 1111
Studio City, CA 91604
tel. 818.379.8799
fax 818.986.3408
mw@mwp.com
www.mwp.com

Cover Design: Johnny Ink
Book Layout: Gina Mansfield Design
Editor: Paul Norlen

Printed by McNaughton & Gunn, Inc., Saline, Michigan
Manufactured in the United States of America

Library of Congress Cataloging-in-Publication Data

Chitlik, Paul, 1947-
A step-by-step guide to strengthen structure, characters, and drama in
your screenplay / Paul Chitlik.
p. cm.
Includes bibliographical references and index.
ISBN 978-1-932907-39-1
1. Motion picture authorship. 2. Editing. I. Title.
PN1996.C54 2008
808.2'3--dc22
2007036236

Mixed Sources
Product group from well-managed
forests and other controlled sources
www.fsc.org   Cert no. SW-COC-002283
© 1996 Forest Stewardship Council
FSC

For Sophia,
who taught me
what love is

———

TABLE
OF CONTENTS

ACKNOWLEDGMENTS

Teachers often learn more from their students than vice versa, and I thank all my students for what they have taught me. I especially thank one, Terry Holdredge, for encouraging me to write this book. He even went so far as to outline my lectures and give me a preliminary table of contents. The pressure!

I also want to thank Jim Schmerer, Richard Walter, Stephanie Moore, and Hal Ackerman of UCLA for their encouragement, support, and words of wisdom. Thanks go to my crew of trusted advisors for this project — Erica Byrne, Marty Winkler, Elizabeth Hargreaves, and Carri Karuhn. They helped me shape the book and improved its usefulness. Of course, anything they didn't catch or any mistakes I insisted on making anyway are my own fault.

More general career thanks go to Jeffrey Davis, Loyola Marymount University; Linda Venis, UCLA Extension; Marc Sheffler, king of the instant joke; Priscilla's Coffee (my second office); Star Frohman, who always forces me to go deeper; Barbara Alexander, agent extraordinaire; my publishers, Ken Lee and Michael Wiese; and my editor, Paul Norlen.

To avoid confusion, I have used the masculine set of pronouns for when I write about characters within a movie in general. Of course, when they are specifically female characters, I use the feminine set. When writing about readers, producers, writers, development executives, agents, and studio personnel in general, I have used the feminine set of pronouns. It's understood that any of these roles can be played by either gender.

Introduction

All professional screenwriters, and most experienced amateurs, know that no script is ready to shoot after only one draft. It's not at all unusual for a script to go through a dozen or more drafts before it gets to the set (I marked upwards of thirty on one of my own projects), and even then it's not finished. Most professionals wading through the rewrite process, though, have people guiding them: other writers, executive producers and producers, development executives, agents, and managers. But new writers don't have the support system to get them from the "puke draft" to one that is of professional quality and ready to submit.

Beginning screenwriters can refer to Syd Field's *Screenplay*, Richard Walter's *Screenwriting*, or Chris Vogler's *The Writer's Journey*, to name but three of scores of books available to learn the basics of screenwriting. But the real application of craft comes in the rewrite. Only a few books offer any help to the rewriter. Problem is, none is a how-to book that gives specific, step-by-step instructions to the novice writer. None offers a complete, practical approach that guides you through the complete process. Film schools that offer rewriting classes (few schools do) are at a loss for texts. Individuals are on their own.

Rewrite is the new writer's first practical guide to getting through the next draft of his or her screenplay. From self-assessment to restructuring to revoicing, it charts an easy-to-follow, task-specific course through the miasma of the rewrite process. Citing examples of well-known movies and providing periodic To Do assignments, this book makes the difficult journey a little less lonesome and a lot less foreboding. *Rewrite* serves as your development executive, your instructor, and your trusted advisor to guide you through the rewrite process in the absence of direct feedback.

In my twenty-five years as a television and film writer, producer, and director, and my eight years teaching at UCLA and Loyola Marymount University, I have rewritten literally hundreds of teleplays and screenplays and supervised the writing and rewriting of another 700 plus. Here's the first thing I learned about writing: Writing is hard. The second thing I learned: It's not done until it's rewritten. Yes, the torture of getting it down on paper, of facing the blank monitor, is over when you've finished the first draft. You can sit back and feel the warmth of "having written" flow over you. Problem is, because you're not sure of yourself or the process, you don't know what to do next, and that's why desk drawers everywhere are full of manuscripts that will never see the light of day again.

But now it's time to take the diamond in the rough, the block of granite that you have carved out of the quarry of your mind, and turn it into the Star of India or the Pietá. Or, to drop the metaphors, you can take all that ink and paper of your first draft and recycle it, because chances are you won't be able to sell it as is. Or you can possibly turn it into *Chinatown* or *Shakespeare in Love*.

Let's look at it another way. More than 55,000 scripts a year get registered by the Writers Guild of America, West. But studios and production companies (I'm not talking about your friend with the new HD video camera) make only 350 or so films a year. And I can say with absolute certainty that not a single one of them is the real first draft. Every single one was rewritten by the original writer at least once, more likely a dozen times, and quite possibly others have worked it over as well. So the truth is, to go from the 55,000 to the 350, you must pass through rewrite-ville.

But rewrite-ville is not a bad place to be. As a matter of fact, according to writer-director Jane Anderson, writer of *When Billie Beat Bobbie*, *It Could Happen to You*, and *The Positively True Adventures of the Alleged Texas Cheerleader-Murdering Mom*, "It's inevitable that the first draft is a shitty draft." She even goes so far as to recommend writing a terrible first draft on purpose. "It's not a flaw, but part of the process."

This is where the fun can be. This is where, as my friend Vince McKay asserts, "The magic begins." Or, as a student of mine maintains, "This is where the work begins." This is where those great turns of phrase come from. This is where writers choose to tell about character and not just plot information. Jim Schmerer, who heads up UCLA's online Professional Program in Screenwriting and whose television credits range from *Star Trek* to *MacGyver* and way too many more to mention, points out that in *Outbreak*, Lawrence Dworet and Robert Roy Pool, the credited writers, have Dustin Hoffman's character need information from the Coast Guard. A secretary tells him that she has a friend who's in the Coast Guard. In the first draft, Hoffman might have said, "Could you ask him to help?" and that would get across all the information he needs. But he says, "How good a friend?" In the final draft, the secretary answers, "Better than his wife would like," which tells us both that she can get the information as well as something about her character.

That's the kind of double hit you can create in rewriting that, while you're buzzing through a first draft, you don't have time to think about.

But there's much, much more craft involved. Now's the time to see if what you had in mind got put down on the page. Now's the time when you take the block of granite and chip away at everything that *isn't* the Pietá. Now's when you hone and polish, expand and contract, build and shape. It's more fun now that the page isn't blank. It's more thoughtful and artful. But if you don't have a mentor, or a studio executive, or a director to give you "notes," where do you start?

You start with this book. With your screenplay on one side of the desk, and this book on the other, you follow a clear process that will help you analyze your screenplay, identify strengths and weaknesses, and create a course of action, a blueprint, for your rewrite.

A truism of screenplay writing is that rewriting is hard. Rewriting on your own is even harder. *Rewrite* is like having your own rewrite mentor so you don't have to go through the process by yourself. Each chapter has To Dos, practical exercises that relate directly to your current screenplay but that also give you a method to use in the future. For best results, do them as you go along, but feel free to read the whole book through before writing anything new.

The order I have set out in this book is the order I suggest to my students, but just as every writer approaches the rewrite from a different angle, doing different things in different orders, you can read and use this book anyway that suits you.

One rule about screenwriting: There are no rules. There are guidelines that have worked for a hundred years (and 2,500 years before that in play writing), but there are no rules. So, if at any point you disagree with me, do what you feel is best and see if it works. If it does, good. If it doesn't, try it my way and see what you get. Chances are it'll work my way, because my way isn't my way, it's the way most screenwriters and development executives in Hollywood approach the screenplay today.

Which brings up another issue. We're talking about Hollywood movies here. We're not talking about *Jules et Jim*, *Shoot the Piano Player*, *Los olvidados*, *Belle Epoch*, or *The Apu Trilogy*. Of course, some of what I'm about to lay out here works for those films, but not everything. I don't know how to write for French New Wave Cinema, Italian Post-War Realism, Spain pre- or post-Franco, or India after the Raj. They're good films that continue to touch the lives of their countrymen, and even us lowly Americans, but they're foreign to most American audiences in structure, approach, and content, and thus unacceptable to most Hollywood studios and production companies. And, I assume, the goal is to make a film that American studios will buy and American audiences will appreciate.

If, however, the goal is to make the best indie film out there, you'll still do better rewriting your film with my guidelines than trying to copy the form of *Last Year at Marienbad* (even if you could figure it out, and I couldn't and I read the book!). A good indie film still needs good structure, good characters, good dialogue, good action.

So let's get started on that rewrite.

But wait. How long is this process going to take? If you have no other responsibilities and can work full time on it, it could take from a few weeks to a couple of months. If you have a job and a family, maybe three to four months working ten hours per week. Adjust your time frame accordingly.

Writers are notorious for procrastinating. I suggest you do the same, but with a plan. I usually straighten out my office, vacuum the house, go for a bike ride, and take in the dry cleaning. Whatever you're going to do, write it down, then do it. Don't add to the list. When you've finished, you're ready. Mind clear, spirit willing. Then come back to Chapter One.

CHAPTER 1

CLARIFYING
STORY AND STRUCTURE
FOR IMPACT

When a developer decides to build a skyscraper, one of the first things he does, after researching and selecting the site, is to hire an architect to design the structure. He knows that a builder, no matter how experienced or educated, can't construct a high-rise without blueprints. The blueprints will detail the entire project from the depth of the foundation to the size and color of the tiles in the men's room. The plans enable the hundreds of people working to realize the project to have the same vision, to be in agreement on process and result. Not that there isn't opportunity for change (if you've ever remodeled your house you know about change orders) or creative collaboration. But everyone works from a common plan.

In film and television, that common plan is the script. Everyone from the props person to the lead actor relies on that document for guidance, so it is a technical document as well as a literary one. And, just as with blueprints, there are certain conventions that everyone relies on. One is a reliance on story.

If movies are all about characters and their goals, what characters do when faced with barriers to these goals is the story. To define story in the simplest way: There's a person. He has a goal. There's a wall between him and the goal. He has to go over, under, around, or through the wall to get to his goal.

That's the story. That's the plot of your movie — the process of getting to the goal. The goal may change. The wall may take various forms (both inside your protagonist and outside of him). But the fact remains, story is the character striving towards his goal.

There's an expression of this form in dramatic terms that has worked for thousands of years: the three-act structure. This has been refined in the last hundred years of movie making and can be summed up in seven specific points of your movie, all of which relate to the protagonist's goal.

This seems like the starting point for thinking about your movie, but it's not the only one. My philosophy, shared by thousands of other writers (but by no means all), is that movies begin with character. Of course, what befalls the character or what the character does in pursuit of his goal are what movies are about as well. But I chose to start the book by discussing structure because you can't discuss character without discussing structure, and I didn't want to have to define my terms twice.

I encourage you to flip back and forth between the chapters much like a professor would jump between subjects in a lecture. Remember that character is action, action is character. So the very act of pursuing a goal is how you define your character. It's all intertwined.

So, let's see if your script has the seven points that provide the bare bones of the body of your movie. The points:

1. Ordinary life: getting to know who the central character is and what his issue (flaw) is. We see the protagonist in his usual surroundings, dealing with the usual people in his life, but we also see that he has some issues and that there is a need for change. He may or may not know that.

In *Thelma & Louise,* written by Calli Khouri, for example, Thelma starts off as the repressed housewife to car salesman/ district manager Darryl, a male chauvinist pig if there ever was one. She even has to ask his permission to go away for the weekend. Her first act of rebellion comes when Thelma calls Louise back and tells her the pick-up time.

This is a film full of montages. The first long one is Thelma packing. But the point of this montage is to show her packing way too much stuff (which will lead to conclusions by the cop, Hal Slocumb, much later) and to note that she packs a gun with distaste. How she handles the gun later will also demonstrate how far she's come on her journey.

Once she's in the car and has handed over the gun to Louise, she hears some fateful words: "You get what you settle for." Apparently, she's settled for Darryl. If she ever wants to get rid of him, we infer, she's got to do something about it. Her condition is clear. Her issues are clear.

We have no idea what we're in for while we watch the opening credits of *In & Out*, screenplay by Paul Rudnick. The location is set up by a series of local "beauty shots" as we're in-troduced to the "great big small town" of Greenleaf, Indiana, that Howard Brackett (Kevin Kline) lives in. This is a heart and soul town, the kind of town that made America strong and rich. The kind where the values haven't changed since it was settled in the 1800s. Or so it would seem.

When we meet Howard, he's in the classroom, his milieu, reciting a Shakespearean sonnet. We can sense his enthusiasm for Shakespeare. He makes his students laugh. He tolerates their questions about a former student, Cameron Drake (Matt Dillon), who's up for an Academy Award. When a nervous student gives him a letter to open from Indiana University, we understand his level of commitment to his students, and his students' admiration of him. He's a likeable guy. If we weren't already convinced, when his buddies shower him with champagne because of his upcoming wedding to Emily Montgomery (Joan Cusack), we're positive. Everyone likes Mr. Brackett.

And everyone knows Howard's life is about to change, but they have no idea how much, and neither do we. We think he's about to get married to a woman he's been engaged to for years. She tries on her dress with Howard and his mother, Berniece (Debbie Reynolds).

But what's the issue? The issue is subtextual. Why has this purportedly heterosexual man not had sex with his fiancé of three years? Why has he not admitted that he's gay? Does he even know?

2. The inciting incident: usually around page 15 (or 15 minutes into the film), give or take a couple of pages. Something happens to your protagonist that will change his life forever. Eventually, it will compel him to act. It will help him define his goal.

In *Thelma & Louise*, they make a stop at a country bar, and the drinking begins. Louise is a little hesitant, but Thelma reminds her, "You said we were gonna have some fun, so let's have some." Thelma starts dancing with a stranger who fills her full of beer and spins her 'til she's dizzy. When he takes her outside for some "air," he forces himself on her. Soon, it's a full-fledged rape and beating, eventually stopped by Louise pulling the trigger on Thelma's gun and putting a hole in the man's heart.

Now that's an inciting incident!

Their lives are definitely going to change now.

In *In & Out,* there are two things exciting in town: Howard's imminent wedding and Cameron's Oscar possibilities. These two converge during the Academy Awards presentation itself when, after some very funny scenes from the war movie Cameron was nominated for and some insider jokes by Glenn Close, Cameron wins the award. In his acceptance speech, he thanks Howard, his high school drama teacher, and then says, quite without necessity, that the teacher is gay. In a gesture he thinks is a tribute, he dedicates the night to Howard Brackett. Things are never going to be the same for Howard Brackett again.

Emily, Howard's fiancée, is confused. "Howard, what's he talking about?" Of course, had she thought about it, she might have guessed. A three-year engagement devoid of sex. Barbara Streisand movies. Disco music. In the nutty world Rudnick has created, it all adds up.

Now the film has a purpose. Now it's rolling. Because that's what an inciting incident does — it changes the life of the protagonist forever. It forces him to seek a goal he may not have thought of, or, if he'd thought of it, never had the courage to pursue. In this case, it wreaks havoc on Howard's life. How can he get married if he's gay? It's news to his mother, his father, his fiancée.

And Howard claims it's news to him, too. He's not gay, no no, not him. He's just about to get married, for cryin' out loud.

3. **End of Act One**: when your character decides on a course of action in order to deal with whatever the inciting incident brought up. Usually, another major event forces him to decide that he must take action. A plan is part of that. This usually occurs between pages 25 and 35. Now your character has a goal, and your story has focus.

Thelma calls Darryl at four in the morning, and he isn't there. She starts to understand maybe she's the one who should be upset about her spouse's behavior instead of vice versa. After Louise decides they should go to Mexico, Thelma has a conversation with Darryl, but he's too busy with his football game. He makes an idle threat, and she tells him to "go fuck yourself." Her attitude is changing.

Thelma decides to go to Mexico and learns about Louise's past run in with the law in Texas. Now she asks how long it will take to get to Mexico. She states her goal. That's the end of Act One.

In *In & Out*, the pronouncement begins to create doubts in certain minds, but its ramifications are ominous when the principal, played by Bob Newhart, warns Howard to prove himself straight and get married. His students, the ones on his team, begin to doubt him and turn modest when he enters the locker room. Even his buddies at his own bachelor party are thrown for a loop. And then the priest counsels him to "be" with his fiancée. He rushes to Emily and tries to make love to her only to be freaked out by a Richard Simmons video. This inciting incident has created chaos in his life. He's got to do something about it. What? By the end of the act, Howard's mission is clear — he has to get married and prove that he's not gay.

4. **Midpoint or turning point**. Yes, this does happen right around the middle wherein the action takes a sudden and new unexpected direction. The goal may change. The

central character may realize what his flaw is. His true needs become more important than what he wants.

Jimmy, Louise's boyfriend, is waiting for Louise at the hotel where he was supposed to wire her the money. She gives the money to Thelma for safekeeping, and we should know by now that something's going to go wrong with that, but we don't know what. When J. D. (Brad Pitt) comes to Thelma's door, all wet and seductive, Thelma takes him in and her life really changes. Darryl and she had been together since she was fourteen. He was the only man she ever knew. Now she learns a thing or two about sex with J. D. As a matter of fact, she's light headed and drunk with sex the next morning. That is, until Louise asks her where the money is. J. D. has stolen it. Now the story spins off in a new direction. Thelma wants to maintain that "It's okay," but Louise says, "It's not okay. None of this is okay."

Up to this point, Thelma has been pulled along by events. She hasn't yet propelled the action by design, though what has happened to her has propelled the action. But now she has to take action. She takes charge. The action spins off in a new and unexpected direction. The women go on a crime spree!

Just before the middle of *In & Out*, Howard is still determined to prove that he is not gay. In a masterpiece visual, he literally bumps into the one person who can help him, at, not coincidentally, a crossroads.

The catalyst for his self-discovery is Peter Molloy, played by Tom Selleck, an out-of-the-closet journalist who just won't let the story go. He forces Howard to come to terms with himself. How? By knocking him over at an intersection — literally the crossroads of his life. By kissing him full on the mouth and making him accept the fact that he likes it.

Now Howard's task is to come to grips with the fact that he's gay. The story spins off in a different direction. His goal is different.

5. The low point: end of the second act. The all-is-lost point in terms of the goal. It appears there's no way in hell he'll ever reach his goal. Happens around page 75-85 depending on the length of the script.

In *Thelma & Louise*, Darryl can't believe it when the FBI and Hal show him the tape of Thelma's convenience store robbery, but Thelma thinks she may have "found her calling" (armed robbery). Hal later questions J.D. and asks him if he thinks Thelma would have robbed the store if he hadn't stolen their money, and it's clear he thinks they're just victims of circumstance. When Louise and Thelma next call Darryl, Louise asks him to put the cops on; and Hal takes the phone. He wants them to turn themselves in to him; he knows they're going to Mexico.

This is the low point of the film, the end of the second act. Nothing's going well. Louise says the only thing they had going for them was that the cops didn't know where they were going. And now they know. They're frightened, but determined. They head off into the night.

Things are no better for Howard by now. He's finally at the wedding, still not owning up. At the altar, doubts creep in, and he admits to Emily, and to the world, that he's gay. He should be relieved, but he's not. He's flustered, confused. Peter congratulates him and gets clocked in the jaw for his trouble. Howard's life is over.

But the ultimate low point takes place off camera and Howard relates it to his father, who has come over after the aborted wedding. Howard's been fired because he's gay. Everything he ever worked for is out the window. He's devastated the woman he loves (not in *that* way, but loves nonetheless). How's he ever going to regain his life?

6. The final challenge. At the beginning of Act Three, your protagonist sees something, hears something, or even remembers something that reanimates him and gives him the will to continue. Then he prepares to face the final test, the final barrier that your character must overcome in order to reach his goal. The last, biggest battle. The run across Manhattan to proclaim his love. The final struggle to the summit. The last ten yards. This occurs very close to the end of your film.

Once Thelma and Louise have been located, their fate is sealed. Or appears to be. They could give themselves up, or they could turn and fight. But either way they'd lose, and neither way would be on their terms. If there's anything that Thelma's learned, it's that she now has control, and has to keep control, of her own life. She tells Louise she is a good friend. On the edge of the Grand Canyon, with no escape possible, Louise says she's not going to give up. Thelma suggests that they don't get caught. They should keep on goin'. She points to the edge of the canyon. Louise: "You sure?" Thelma: "Yeah." They kiss, start the car, hold hands, and fly into the canyon.

That's her final challenge, and she reaches her goal. She's completely free now.

Howard Brackett should be receiving the teacher of the year award, but now he can't because he's gay. But his family and his students and the rest of the community aren't about to let that happen, so in a Spartacus moment — "I am Spartacus. I am Spartacus." — everyone admits to being gay. Howard is vindicated for coming out, life returns to normal, and everyone is accepted for who they are.

Only problem is, Howard is not the agent of his own salvation. Yes, he came out, but he didn't really stand up for himself and fight the principal. This is an example of having the cavalry make a last-minute rescue, and it's one of the failings of the film. Had Howard fought, the finish would have been much stronger.

7. The return to (the now-changed-forever) **normal life**. Two or three pages to show us that life goes on and that our character has triumphed and changed.

It could be argued that there is not a return to a now-changed forever normal life in *Thelma & Louise*. They're dead. But what could be a greater change than that? The slide show of their journey underscores that they had the time of their lives. And now their lives are over. But Thelma went on an incredible journey of self-discovery and change. The implication is that it's the audience that is going to return to a now-changed-forever life because of Thelma and Louise's journey. They may never look at men in the same way again.

For Howard, there must be a moment of *normal gay life*. In this case, it's the renewal of vows that his parents make with him and his presumed "date," Peter (the newsman), looking on. There's no drastic external change. He'll still teach. He'll still be popular in town. It's just that he's gay now.

GUIDELINES, NOT LAWS

The seven points are only guidelines, of course. But the inciting incident should come as early as you can get it while still showing us who the main character is and why we should care about him. All points after that are in relation to the character's goal. (See Appendix A for a compressed version of the seven points of *Thelma & Louise*.)

There are scenes between these points — important scenes — and many barriers to get through and many people to relate to, but these are the major signposts along the way of your protagonist's journeys. I say journeys, because the story is only one of the journeys. The protagonist is really on three journeys: the "A" story — the plot; the "B" story — the relationship; and the "C" story — the internal journey dealing with the flaw. And every one of these stories has a seven-point structure. And every point along each of these journeys is defined in terms of the goal: reaching the story goal; creating or mending a relationship and thus reaching the emotional goal; changing into a better person (learning something about life that will help him), and thus reaching the personal development goal.

These journeys are intertwined and interdependent. Often, a plot point for the A story serves as the same point in the B or C story. In fact, the better integrated the three stories, the better the screenplay.

To Do

Briefly outline your story in terms of the seven points. Write no more than a sentence about each of the seven points. Make sure that each point after the inciting incident relates to the goal of your central character.

When you've done all that, come back here. There's more to do on story.

THE BEATSHEET

It's possible your story is out of balance or is missing some of the points. Now's the time to really see where you are in your structure. Were all your points expressed in terms of the protagonist's goal? Were they in proximity to the balance described above? Now we're going to get intimate with your script. Without making any changes in your story yet, we need to see exactly what you have in terms of scenes, so let's write a beatsheet of your story.

If you're like most professional screenwriters, you didn't just sit down and start to write your screenplay. You thought about it, you wrote notes, you may have even done some character sketches. And, if you followed procedure, you at least did a beatsheet, if not a complete treatment (that's the subject of another book). A beatsheet is a list of the scenes of your story. Every writer does it differently, but most write at least a line or two to remind them what each scene will be (see Appendix B for a sample beatsheet). But the beatsheet you wrote when you started your script might not correspond to what ended up in your script. You may have added scenes, changed them, taken some away. That's the process. When you're writing the beatsheet, it's easy to shift scenes around, insert new ones, take out ones that don't really move the story.

When you do your rewrite, you've got to be ready to do this, too, so you need a new beatsheet to get the lay of the land. The best way to do this, according to some screenwriters, is to write each beat on an index card. Then shuffling is a cinch. But with the way computers work these days most screenwriting programs give you the ability to do the same thing, so you can choose. But whatever way you choose, it will help you to do that now. This will take some time, but don't worry, I'm patient. Come back when you've got a one-line description of each scene including who's in it and what the conflict or character point is of that scene (more on what should be in a scene in Chapter Four). Do not include transitions such as riding in a car or establishing shots. Number each beat for convenience. The beatsheet will probably be three single-spaced pages or so, with anywhere from 30-75 scenes. I'll wait here while you do that.

DEVELOPING SUBPLOTS

You're back. Good. Let's talk about subplots, because they're easier to talk about than to layer into your story. You should, by this time, be thinking of the two main subplots — that is, the "B" and the "C" story — the emotional subplot and the personal growth subplot. In most stories, the central story is the "A" story. In romantic comedies, it's the emotional, or "B," story.

There are others, too, because there are always other things going on in a protagonist's life — he could have a story with the barista at the local Starbucks; there could be something happening with his dog; he might have an issue with his floor wax. These should reflect his main issue in some way, but don't necessarily have to.

The protagonist is not the only person in your movie. He has friends, lovers, enemies. Each of these people can have a subplot of his own. The more important supporting characters can have a story with the seven points. Lesser characters can have stories that merely have a beginning, middle, and end, so three story points are all that are needed. But the main issue here is, do the subplots somehow illuminate or reflect any of the central character's stories or issues? If they don't, you'll need to ask yourself why you need them.

RAISING THE STAKES

If the biggest, hardest barrier to your protagonist reaching his goal comes at the beginning of the story, where do you go from there? It would be all downhill, and not very suspenseful. So you've got to set up your story so that at each step, it gets harder and harder for your protagonist to get past the obstacles in his way. But there's more.

What is the penalty if your central character doesn't achieve a short-term and, eventually, the long-term goal? In other words, what are the stakes? What is the jeopardy for the protagonist? If he drives too fast, his car will slide off the road. If he fails a test, he'll have to start all over again. If he forces himself on the girl, he'll lose her.

Or his life.

The consequences of failure should be dire in terms of your character. He could lose a fortune. He could lose his house, his children, or his job. The country or world could be destroyed. Whatever it is, it has to be worthy of our attention. Going after a goal that is not worthy will make your audience not care enough. If they don't care, they won't watch.

And as you progress in your script, you should be continually raising the stakes. Do you?

To Do

What happens to your central character if he fails in his quest? What are the consequences of failure? Write one or two lines describing the stakes.

THE BARRIERS

Some words of reminder about barriers — they come from within and they come from without. The barrier within is your protagonist's flaw. It's what will prevent him from achieving his goal unless he overcomes it. So we need to be reminded what that flaw is, and we need to see it affect the outcome of attempts to overcome barriers. In other words, you have to set up learning situations for your protagonist. Have you?

And have you set up situations where the antagonist force is making life difficult for your protagonist? Again, ask yourself, is it tough to reach the goal or is it easy? It had better be tough. The tougher the better.

WHO IS THE REAL HERO?

One of the most difficult things about writing a feature film is to figure out who the hero is. Yes, hero. Even in a romantic comedy. Even in a teen sex romp. Even in a horror picture, there is a hero. The hero is the person who has to overcome adversity to reach his goal. And he must be the person who does this in the final challenge (sometimes called the climax). In other words, the main character must be the agent of his own salvation. The cavalry can't come riding in at the last minute (as it does in *Fort Apache*). His best friend can't save him. A virus can't save the world from Martian invaders (one of the main flaws of *War of the Worlds*). It has to be the protagonist who fights and perseveres and overcomes whatever final barriers there are between him and his goal (Luke in *Star Wars*, Dorothy in *The Wizard of Oz*). If not, the audience will be unsatisfied. They might not know why, but they will not be happy with the movie.

To Do

Write in one line what your protagonist does to overcome the big barrier in the final challenge. He can have help, but he must lead the charge, whatever form that charge takes.

You've done some major work in this chapter, so it's time for a little reward. Think of something mindless that you don't ordinarily make time for. An hour reading the newspaper at Starbucks. Bowling a couple of frames. A trip to the library for no reason at all. I like to exercise after completing a stage in a rewrite, so I'd be on my mountain bike by now, challenging the Verdugo Mountains. Go do something other than writing (or even thinking). Then come back.

CHAPTER 2

THE
POWERFUL
PROTAGONIST

"Character is the fundamental material we are forced to work with, so we must know character as thoroughly as possible."
— Lajos Egri, *The Art of Dramatic Writing*

Movies are not abstractions like modern art. They are based on people: their interactions, their responses to conflict, their emotions. The building blocks of movies are characters: interesting, vital, dynamic, funny, weird, scary, stupid, bizarre characters. And every movie is the story of one person's emotional (and often physical) journey. Notice I said "one person's."

Students frequently ask me if there can be more than one central character. What about *Butch Cassidy and the Sundance Kid*? What about *Thelma & Louise*? The answer to that is they are buddy pictures, but there still is one buddy who is dominant, around whom the story revolves. In *Butch* it's Butch. In *T&L*, it's Thelma (does placement in the title give you a hint?). But what about ensemble movies? I usually ask, "Like which ensemble movies?" A sharp class will come up with one: *The Big Chill*. A really sharp class will add another: *The Secaucus Seven*. And maybe *The Breakfast Club*. (*Ocean's Eleven* isn't.) Then you're done. And even if you could come up with more, they would still be the exception. And even though there are no rules, audiences find it confusing to deal with more than one central character. And since a movie is defined by the journey of one character, it's important to figure out who the central character is before you go any further.

That's why I'm going to tell you about the single most important thing you must know about your central character, your protagonist: "What does he want?" Though this may change later to "What does he need?", it is the driving force of the movie. It defines your character. It motivates the action. Everything that happens in the movie happens because your central character is pursuing a goal. That's what pushes the action. That's what causes the changes. That's what tells us who the character is. So, do you have the right protagonist for your movie, and do you know what he wants?

MATCHING CHARACTER TO PREMISE

The first thing we have to ask before reviewing our characters is what is this movie about? What is its premise? Then we can make sure our central character proves this premise. By premise, I'm talking about Egri's definition of premise — the central thesis of the movie, what you are setting out to prove. It could be "Great love defies even death," as it is in *Titanic* (and *Romeo and Juliet*). It could be "Greed destroys the soul," as it is in *Treasure of the Sierra Madre* (and *The Merchant of Venice*).

CHARACTERS COME OUT OF PREMISE.
PREMISE COMES FROM CHARACTERS

Premise is the underlying message that you're trying to sneak into your movie. You do want to really say something as well as entertain, don't you? Executives will quote you Samuel Goldwyn's line, "If you want to send a message, use Western Union," but, really, if a film is not about something, it's not going to be worth watching. Even the simplest films have a premise. (You might call it a theme, an idea, a subject, whatever term you want. Egri calls it premise.)

The premise is usually expressed in one line and doesn't contain the words *is* or *are* (which merely state definitions). Some premises from contemporary films: "Underestimating nature leads to disaster" for *The Perfect Storm*. "Right conquers tyranny" for *The Patriot*. "Cooperation and hope will free you from bondage" from *Chicken Run*. Yes, *Chicken Run*. "With great power comes great responsibility" from *Spider Man*.

So, before we go any further in the exploration of character, think about what you are really trying to say with your story. I'm not talking about a one-line summary of the action. I'm talking about the message that underlies everything, the deepest core of the movie.

To Do

Write your premise now. Do not use the words *is* or *are*. Do not tell the story, only the idea of the truth you want to prove.

MATCHING THE CHARACTERS TO THE PREMISE

Once you have an idea of what your movie is about, you must make sure the characters you have will help you prove your premise. When you first write your movie you can find the characters and then look for a premise. It's harder to do it that way. I've done it, and so have lots of other people. But if you know what your characters have to achieve ahead of time, it makes it easier to find the kind of characters you need. But you already have your characters, so let's make sure they're a good match.

For example, in *Romeo and Juliet*, if Romeo had been thoughtful and cautious, say like Hamlet, the story would have gone nowhere. The premise of "Great love defies even death" would never have been proven with Hamlet as the central character. If George Clooney's character, Captain Billy Tyne, had been cautious, there would have been no story in *The Perfect Storm*.

The personalities of these characters drove these stories. Their actions proved the premises. And only these characters would have worked.

Maybe you're thinking that these characters created these plots, and you would be right. Certainly without the Clooney character, there is no plot, just a big storm. Without the Mel Gibson character's background, without his love for his family, without his slip into a killing frenzy, there would be no *The Patriot*. Without Alvy Singer's nebbish personality and quirky sense of humor, there would be no *Annie Hall*. What would *Bill and Ted's Excellent Adventure* be without Bill and Ted? *Groundhog Day* without the cynical Phil Conners? *Tootsie* without the grating, difficult to work with Michael Dorsey?

So, does your character help prove your premise? Is he a good match?

CHARACTER CONSTRUCTION

Let's find out who your character is to make sure he's the right one for your premise. If he isn't, we can adjust him... or the premise. How do we find out? By deconstructing him. You have a person in mind, but can the audience see him clearly? They will if you know your character.

Lajos Egri, in *The Art of Dramatic Writing*, says there are three components to every character: the physiological, the sociological, and the psychological. In other words, what they look like physically; where they come from and what their circumstances are now; and what their thought processes and emotions are. It's also good to include their goals and the flaws or quirks that set them apart. For example, let's look at the Mel Gibson character, Benjamin Martin, in *The Patriot*, written by Robert Rodat:

The Ghost, Benjamin Martin
Physiology: 40s. Dark hair. Rugged looking. In good shape.

Sociology: Plantation owner, but does not own slaves. Widower. Father of six. Former army captain. Legislator. Famous.

Psychology: Suffers from post-traumatic stress as a result of the French and Indian War. Afraid that sins would revisit him. (And they do). Slow to anger, but a mighty temper. Failed furniture maker, but doesn't give up. Sentimental. Soft spoken. Pacifist until forced. Family, freedom, and frenzy would be an accurate short list of his concerns.

Flaw that he must overcome: His blood lust.

Goal: To stay out of war> To rescue son> To win war.

Or, let's look at George Bailey, from *It's a Wonderful Life* (screenplay by Frances Goodrich, Albert Hackett, and Frank Capra, additional scenes by Jo Swerling, based on a story by Phillip Van Doren Stern):

George Bailey
Physiology: Starts as a child. Loses hearing (after saving brother). Grows tall and slender.

Sociology: Middle class, intact family. Father is the head of a savings and loan (George goes to his office). Has a maid. Has a younger brother whom he saves. Works in a drug store as a child, takes over father's business. People like him (Mary whispers into his ear; the other girl likes him, too). Lives in a small town. Never gets to college or to travel.

Psychology: Interested in travel, adventure. Willing to risk life to save others. Compassionate. Speaks his mind. Happy and not afraid to show it. Loves his father. Loyal. Sincere. Patriotic.

Flaw: Has a temper.

Goal: To do something big and important.

The more you know about your central character, the better you will write him or her. As you rewrite, you may be putting your character into new situations with new people, and you'll need to know who he is in order to write his behavior and dialogue and to make him consistent throughout the story. Also, when the time comes to rewrite his dialogue, you'll be more conversant with who your protagonist is, so his speech and actions will flow more freely from your fingertips.

To Do

Write a profile of your central character.

Name:

Physiology (including age):

Sociology:

Psychology:

Goal:

Personality Flaw That Hinders Him:

MOTIVATION

Now you have a clear idea of who your character is. The clearer your picture of him, the clearer you'll be able to express him in print and the better you'll be able to motivate his actions. Knowing where he comes from, both physically and mentally, will tell you where he's going. Now he has reasons to do things, not just for the convenience of the story, but organically. What your character does in response to the challenges in your story is who your character is. John Sacret Young, co-creator of *China Beach* and writer of *Testament* and *Romero* says, "Problems come up when you don't know the character well enough."

CONSISTENCY

The next thing to check for is consistency. Is your character consistent in his responses throughout your script, or does he sometimes do things that are "out of character"? Sure, he can do surprising things, so long as they make sense within the character that you have constructed. Alvy Singer wouldn't lift weights in his spare time. Michael Dorsey wouldn't take an insult calmly. Hannibal Lecter wouldn't use bad grammar — except for effect.

To Do

Go through your script and make sure your central character acts consistent with the personality you've given him. Ensure that each action and each word make sense for the character's physiology, sociology, and psychology.

MAKING YOUR CHARACTER WATCHABLE

You know in the first five minutes whether you like a movie or not. A major part of that is how you feel towards the central character. In most Hollywood movies, that means either we like him or he's so intensely interesting that he compels our attention. Think about it. How many films are successful that have unredeemed jerks as their central character? Sure, you can name a couple of exceptions — try *Scarface* or even *The Godfather: Part II*.

But they are the exceptions, and they feature intensely interesting people. But even in movies where the protagonist starts out as a jerk, he usually ends up as something else. Think of Jim Carrey's character, Fletcher Reede, in *Liar Liar*, written by Paul Guay and Stephen Mazur. Even though he's despicable in many ways at the beginning of the story, there's something we like about him — he loves his son and he's funny. (It helps that Mazur is a world-class wisecracker.)

In other movies it can be the character's sense of humor, looks, or vulnerability that win us over. Most of all, though, it's their flaws and quirks that make us identify with the protagonist. Flaws make a character more interesting. The good guy has some bad qualities. That makes him human. Approachable. Believable. Part of his conflict is fighting those qualities.

Nick Kazan, writer of *Frances*, *Reversal of Fortune*, and *Bicentennial Man*, among others, puts it this way: The character doesn't have to be likeable, just compelling. The reader/viewer has to be able to see themselves as that person. "As long as he is emotionally true," Kazan says, "then you're on the ride."

To Do

What makes your character watchable? Notice, I didn't say likeable. Write that in one sentence or less.

If you don't have a good answer for that, go back and rethink your character sketch. Whatever you come up with, you will have to incorporate into the sketch and then into the script.

THE GOAL

This is the single most important thing you must know about your protagonist. If a character has no goal, then he's passive, and the world works on him. He's nobody. He's rolling with the punches. He's not active. He's not central. He's not pushing the action; he's being pulled by it. The word protagonist can be defined in several ways — one in the theatrical way meaning the leading character or hero. But it can also be defined as a person who champions a cause. Your leading character must champion a cause, even if it's his own. He *must* have a goal.

But he doesn't usually have one at the beginning of your movie. He doesn't know what he wants, not until something happens to him at the inciting incident which will compel him to develop a goal. By the end of Act One, though, he will know what that goal is, and he'll have a plan to pursue it. Changes may happen in the middle of Act Two to force him to change that goal, or to realize that his inner need is a more important goal, but the pursuit of a goal will be foremost in his mind throughout the film.

So as a writer, you must know what the goal is and what that goal changes to. You must ensure that he's driving towards that goal in every scene. That's what pushes him.

To Do

What is the apparent goal of your protagonist? What does that goal change to at the midpoint? (In other words, what does he *really* want and need?)

THE FLAW

But there's something that prevents him from reaching that goal. Yes, there's an antagonist, be it Mother Nature as in *The Perfect Storm*, or a Federal marshal as in *The Fugitive*. More on that later. But there's another very powerful force that hinders his progress towards his goal, one that he must overcome in order to reach it, and that's his personality flaw.

DEVELOPING THE FLAW

Nobody's perfect. You've heard that said a million times. You've even used it as an excuse yourself. But you know it to be true.

You've never met a perfect individual, not even your significant other. Not even your perfect child. Not even Superman. Sure, Superman has a physical weakness — he's allergic to kryptonite. But physical flaws don't count. We're talking about personality, even psychological, flaws. Superman never shows his true self. He leads a double life. He finds it hard to connect with people. He's flawed. In short, Superman is human, too.

People will not want to watch your story if your characters aren't human, especially your central character. And to be human, he must be flawed. Shy. Arrogant. Emotionally unavailable. Impetuous. Lacking in confidence. Lacking in social graces. Lacking in maturity. And any one of these or a hundred other flaws can make your protagonist's journey difficult. The flaw is the thing inside himself that your protagonist must overcome in order to defeat the thing outside himself that stands between him and his goal. As Anderson says, "Filling out imperfect people is easier than making a perfect character interesting."

So, again, go to your sketch. Think about the psychological traits your character has. Know what your character's baggage is. What is their loss? Think of the flaws he has. Which one is standing between him and his goal? Which one do you need to emphasize from the very first time we see the protagonist so we know what the issue is he faces? That's the second most important thing you must know about your character. It's the one that gets in the way of the first most important thing (the Goal).

To Do

What in your central character's persona (anger, insecurity, arrogance, greed, inability to connect or commit, selfishness, etc.) is preventing him from reaching his goal? How does this stop him?

REVEALING ACTION THROUGH CHARACTER

How many times have you heard people who talk about writing

say, "Action is character"? What does that mean? It's simple. We define people by what they do (and what they say). Just telling us that a person is charismatic doesn't help in a movie, but showing us how that person uses his magnetism to influence people does (John Wayne in *Fort Apache* or a score of other movies). You can't tell your audience that a character is shy, you must show him in a situation where his actions tell us he is shy (Superman meeting Lois Lane). As a last resort, you can have people talk about him and tell each other he's shy, but nothing works like showing him in a situation where he hides from someone he's afraid to meet or is silent when someone flirts with him. Action is character. A person *is* what he does.

Dirty Harry puts a gun to a man's head and threatens him. Superman leaps tall buildings. Dorothy runs away from the farm and her problems. Luke runs away from his farm to save the universe. Thelma packs a gun, handling it gingerly, then later uses the gun to hold up a convenience store. Each action tells us something about the character at that stage of his development. What he does is who he is.

To Do

Write one-line descriptions of three scenes in which your character does something to show who he is. If you don't have these scenes yet, create them.

OTHER WAYS TO REVEAL CHARACTER

It could even be something as simple as wardrobe. What are the two things we most remember about Erin Brockovich? Okay, besides those two. Yes, the way she dressed. Clearly set up by Susannah Grant, with an assist by Richard LaGravenese (and based on the real person), Erin is flamboyant and not at all afraid to show her body. And another notable trait follows suit — she uses flamboyant language as well, and she's not afraid to speak her mind. A character to remember.

DIALOGUE

What a character says and how he says it is important. It's what made the film *Erin Brockovich* rise above a boring legal proceeding. What she says is who she is. One of the first things that tells you about a character is what that character sounds like. His level of education, his place of origin, his state of mind are all reflected in his speech. Think of *Forrest Gump*. Think of *Coal Miner's Daughter*. Captain Kirk in *Star Trek* sounds different than Dr. Spock, who sounds very different than Spike Lee in *She's Gotta Have It* or Easy Rollins in *Devil with a Blue Dress*, or Jimmy Smits in *Mi Familia*.

Dialogue is one way to delineate your characters. This is especially true for your protagonist. He or she should have his own way of talking. And it's not just what they say, but how they say it. You've also probably noticed that your character's voice changed as you got to know him. So it's a good bet to say that he sounds different at the beginning of your story than at the end. So go through the script reading only the protagonist's dialogue. As you go, look for ways to unify the voice of the character, to make it stand out, to make it tell us who your character really is. Does the dialogue tell us who this person is just by the way he talks? In other words, is there a vocabulary he favors? Is his level of education obvious? Do we hear regionalisms (if appropriate) or an accent? Do we hear his age and social register? (Social register refers to the subtle changes we make in our speech according to whom we're talking. We speak one way to a child, another way to a street tough, and a third way to a priest.)

Some screenwriting programs have a feature that will let you print only the "sides" (relevant pages) for any particular character. That will help you focus on your character in context.

To Do

Read through the central character's dialogue without stopping to read other characters so you can hear just the one voice in your head. Make changes as necessary.

For a good example, focus on Shakespeare's dialogue in *Shakespeare in Love*, then read the rest of the script. Here screenwriters Marc Norman and Tom Stoppard clearly delineate all characters with dialogue but do an especially good job with Shakespeare who often speaks as he writes in his plays. There's a unique freshness in his language. No one else sounds like him. Can you say that about your protagonist?

It's not only a matter of how your character speaks, but what he says. Dialogue is at its most interesting when the character's true intent lies under the words he says, in the subtext. A character is flat when he speaks the subtext, saying what he really means or feels.

Subtext is also often found in dialogue when one thing is said but is meant to refer to something else. Who among us hasn't talked about things in front of (our) children that we didn't want them to understand? We talk about, say, how Betty, a very sensuous person, likes to have sex with a range of international partners. We might say that she likes to sample… uh, coffee from many different lands. She likes American "coffee," French "coffee," Turkish "coffee," but really prefers Italian "coffee."

Sometimes a character does this intentionally in the film, sometimes not. When the lynch mob gathers at the jail in *To Kill a Mockingbird* (screenplay by Horton Foote, based on the novel by Harper Lee), Scout, the young daughter of Atticus (Gregory Peck), diffuses the situation by talking to Mr. Cunningham about several things — the hickory nuts he'd brought over, his son, etc. On the surface, she's just trying to be friendly. Deeper than that, she's showing the mob, and Cunningham in particular, that they're all part of a community that relies on each other, that helps each other out, and that her father in particular is a pillar of this community in the truest sense. Cunningham realizes he can't move against Finch now, and he tells the others to come away with him.

Scout didn't try to tell them the underlying truths, she just talked like they were assumed. Foote knew what he was doing, though. The innocence of the text and the child contrast with the menace of the mob.

In a film, this kind of dialogue can keep your audience on its toes and add character to your characters and spark to your scenes. Look at *The Godfather: Part II* (screenplay by Francis Ford Coppola, based on the novel by Mario Puzo), when Tom Hagen, the Robert Duvall character, talks about Roman times with the turncoat Pantangeli, or in *The Big Sleep* (screenplay by William Faulkner based on the novel by Raymond Chandler), when Bogart's character talks to Bacall's character about horse racing. It's not about horse racing at all but, again, about sex. Nor was Duvall having a historical chat about the Romans. He was negotiating Pantangeli's exit strategy — a clean way for him to commit suicide and take care of his family.

To Do
Find places in your screenplay where you can change on-the-nose dialogue into subtextual dialogue.

THE DEFINING LINE

There's one more line of dialogue that is key to your character. It's often called the character line. It's something your protagonist says that really nails who he is and what his journey has been or will be. UCLA's Jim Schmerer tells his students to look for some place in their screenplay where they can have the major character actually reveal himself to the audience. In addition to telling the reader and audience who this person is, it's something that an actor will glom onto, be interested in, when he reads the screenplay. When an actor gets interested, the studios get interested.

For example, in *The Verdict* (screenplay by David Mamet), Paul Newman's character, Frank Galvin, gives us his character in one speech when he says, "I came in here to take your money. (beat) I brought snapshots to show you. So I could get your money. (to Young Priest, waving away document) I can't take it. If I take it. If I take that money I'm lost. I'm just going to be a rich ambulance chaser. (beat; pleading for understanding) I can't do it. I can't take it."

That speech sets up his character and the fight he's about to enter into. Michael's line in *Tootsie,* where he says, "I'm a better man as a woman than I was as a man," tells the audience just how far Michael has come.

In *Dirty Harry* (screenplay by Harry Julian Fink, R. M. Fink, and Dean Riesner), the infamous line that Harry says to a perp to whose head he's holding his pistol has entered the language, but it also tells us a lot about the character. "Make my day" says he's looking for an excuse to shoot the man, that he has his own set of rules to play by, and that he'll do what he needs to do to get what he wants.

Finding the line for your central character will help you to know him better. If you know the underlying reasons for why a character acts the way he does, not the plot points or what he does, but *why* he does it, what's inside that character — what's driving him or her — it impacts each scene in everything he says and does.

If you know this, you will have your audience emotionally involved in the character.

Here's another example. Marlowe in *The Maltese Falcon* (screenplay by John Huston, based on the novel by Dashiell Hammett): It looks like he'll do anything inside or outside the law to reach his goal: money, the falcon. In the final scene, he turns to the woman he loves and tells her he's going to turn her in for killing his partner.

"Don't believe I'm as crooked as they say. It's good for business." At that moment we know he was a moral detective, and everything was geared towards finding out who killed his partner.

Even an antagonist can have a similar line. Doesn't this line — "I'll be back." — sum up Arnold Schwarzenegger's character in *The Terminator* (written by James Cameron and Gale Anne Hurd) completely?

So, as you read through the dialogue for the protagonist, look for a line like this, and, if there isn't one, write one. It will help you focus on who your character is and what he will do.

To Do
Write that one line of dialogue that says it all for your character.

DEVELOPING THE CHARACTER'S CENTRAL EMOTIONAL RELATIONSHIP
We go to watch movies because of the people in the movies. Even movies loaded with special effects have to have people in them, people about whom we care. And it's not just about the people, it's about the people relating to other people. To be more precise, it's about your central character relating to another person.

In every movie, even action movies, there has to be a central emotional relationship. This is one way to humanize your protagonist. It's a way to show his emotional journey as well as his "story" journey (the one focused on his goal). It's a way to relate to the protagonist on a human level and to root for him. It's a way to ground the story in an emotional reality that everyone can understand.

It doesn't have to be a romantic relationship. It can be a buddy relationship as in *Thelma & Louise*. It can be a stand-in father/daughter relationship as in *Million Dollar Baby*. It can be a mentor/student relationship as in *Star Wars*. The point is, there must be an emotional relationship at the core of your movie to give it heart.

There are two forms this emotional relationship can take. Either it is an emotional relationship that must be established or one that must be repaired. Sometimes, this relationship is the center of the movie, as in a romantic comedy such as *The Philadelphia Story*. Sometimes the relationship is the "B" story and serves to support the "A" story, as in *Armageddon*.

Does your story have a key emotional relationship? If it doesn't, now's the time to create one or beef one up. And the emotional relationship should, like your movie, have a beginning, a middle, and an end. As a matter of fact, it should follow the same seven-point paradigm that your "A" story follows (see Chapter One). Often, the story points for your emotional story correspond to the "A" story points, but not always. They'll be close, though, so when you restructure according to Chapter Four, keep that in mind. For now, just focus on the emotional story itself.

To Do
What is the central emotional relationship of your movie?

What are the seven points of its progress? (Refer to the seven story points of Chapter One, but this time only in terms of the central relationship. The points should coincide, or, at least, be in close proximity).

THE ARC DE CHARACTER
If you've spent any time at all in Hollywood — virtual or real

— you've heard the term "character arc." This is an essential term of art that simply means "how does your character change?" As we discussed earlier, your character must have a flaw. The journey to correct that flaw is his character arc. It's what effect the trials and tribulation of the story have on the character of the character. In other words, how does what happen affect our protagonist? How does he change from a pompous, self-centered cynic, like the Bill Murray character in Danny Rubin's *Groundhog Day* (rewrite by Harold Ramis), to the caring, loving man at the end, capable of true despair, and ultimately, true happiness? There's the arc — from A to Z, but with lots of stops along the way. By the way, rent *Groundhog Day* for a look at a truly different way to study a character using the same events over and over but playing for a different effect each time.

Let's look at the protagonist of another modern classic, Thelma (Geena Davis) of *Thelma & Louise*. When we first meet Thelma, she's a suburban housewife seemingly incapable of making a decision without consulting her husband. Her life is out of her control. She's a virtual slave. She has no ambition of her own.

Then, step-by-step, she takes control of her life, first by going away with Louise (Susan Sarandon), then by deciding to really have fun at the roadhouse. But things spin out of control, and she doesn't know how to handle herself until the midpoint when she is emancipated sexually by J. D. (Brad Pitt). Somehow, now she has the power to take her life in her own hands, to become the driver of the story when Louise is in a deep funk, and even to enter into a new vocation — convenience store robber.

In the end, surrounded by men, she chooses a death of freedom and self-determination. It may be a pessimistic ending, but at least it's one she chooses, finally the mistress of her own destiny.

So, does your character change? Did he go from a self-effacing coward to a self-confident hero? The change doesn't have to be that grandiose, but it must be noticeable. And the progress of this "C" story must also have its own structure — at least a beginning, a middle, and an end. And we know, from our discussion above, that your protagonist must overcome his flaw in order to prevail in the final challenge, so we can see that the seven points of the character arc story again fall in line with the seven points of the central story. So, when you go through your script focusing on just the character, make sure that his arc has enough screen time to be essential to the story and that its major points are in line with the goal-driven "A" story.

It's a lot to remember. Feel free to re-read this chapter at any time in the process. The emotional story and the character arc are intimately entwined with the "A" story and are key to giving life to your protagonist.

To Do
Put your emotional story's seven points next to your character arc's seven points and make sure there's a relationship.

MAKING SURE YOUR PROTAGONIST IS ALL YOU WANT HIM TO BE
One of the key ways to get your script from being 110 pages of paper with words on them to becoming ten thousand feet of

celluloid running through a projector (or a file streamed to a theater) is to get a star attached to it. And the only way to do that is to write a part that the star will want to play. That could mean different things for different stars. A comedy specialist, say Jim Carrey, might want to play a serious role, as in *The Cable Guy*. A chameleon like Meryl Streep might want to play an action role as in *The River Wild*. A child star like Macaulay Culkin might want to show he's an adult, as he does in *Sex and Breakfast*. It may just be a showy role, such as the one Jack Nicholson played in *As Good as It Gets*. Or it may be a very earnest and sympathetic figure like the one Will Smith played in *The Pursuit of Happyness*. In any case, you must offer them a role to sink their teeth into, something that will enhance their career, make them look good, or, at least, look like a good actor. How do you do that? By making the protagonist all you want him to be.

To Do

I use this checklist in my classes to make sure my students have fully developed their protagonists. Before you rewrite your central character, complete this list to help give direction to your rewrite.

No indecisive, do-nothing characters (they can be indecisive as a character flaw, but it must be something they overcome in order to reach their goal).

No passive characters (again, passivity may be a flaw they overcome, but that means by taking action). Your protagonist must push the action. The action can't all just "happen" to him. He drives the story.

Does your protagonist have a passion or obsession that drives him or her?

Is he seeking something?

Does the character speak in his own way?

Nobody without flaws.

Nobody without idiosyncrasies.

Your protagonist must have a sense of humor.
We must know the protagonist's surroundings, job, and home.

Characters grow — they have a desire for change. Do yours?

Characters prove your premise.

Know all three components of their make up and test them in action.

Now What?

Now you have a thorough understanding of who your character is, what he wants, how he would act in any particular situation, and how he changes. Now, what's he up against?

But first, it's time for a little break. Take a writing session off and look at a movie that is in the same genre as the one you're working on. Don't take notes. Just let it settle in. Enjoy it. Imagine that you wrote it. Nice, huh?

CHAPTER 3

THE
WORTHY
ANTAGONIST

If there is no barrier for your protagonist, he will achieve his goal immediately. There is no conflict, so there is no story. (Remember the definition of story.) While this may occasionally happen in real life, it is rare that someone achieves a goal without some difficulty. The more difficulty, the sweeter the victory and the more interesting a story to tell.

The same applies to movie life. If there is nothing to overcome, there is no story. The movie's over before it has a chance to start. So there must be something or someone in opposition, something or someone that makes it hard, almost impossible, for your protagonist to reach his goal. Without struggle there is no story, and the bigger the struggle, the better the story.

So your protagonist must have opposition. And the clearest way to put roadblocks in front of your central character is to have another person be in the way. There are some exceptions — nature is antagonist enough for *The Perfect Storm* or *Volcano*. In a war movie, it's the enemy, sometimes personified, but often not.

What is an antagonist? It's a person whose goals are in conflict with the protagonist. It could be a business competitor, a competitor in love, a criminal (if your protagonist is a detective), a detective (if your protagonist is a criminal), anyone who has a reason to be in the way of the protagonist's goal and actively exercises it.

The antagonist is the second most important person in your film. He has to be a worthy opponent because he must provide the most important barrier to the protagonist's drive toward his goal. If he is too weak, then the fight is too small. He must be stronger than the protagonist, better, faster, smarter, even more handsome (in a romantic comedy, at least). His opposition must force the protagonist to rise above himself to reach his goal. He must be a worthy foe. If he's not, there is no movie.

ADDING DEPTH

If your antagonist is a human being, he must have human qualities to avoid being two-dimensional and predictable. A purely evil protagonist is not interesting. Even a man who runs a concentration camp, exterminating people all day long, may return to a loving wife, children, and a dog. A murderer may have a weakness for sweets. A business rival may harbor a secret passion for music — or S & M. This adds depth to the characterization as well as reality. Even Hitler was reputedly kind to his secretary, and there is footage of him playing with his dogs. It makes his evil all the more chilling.

Just as your protagonist must have a flaw, your antagonist must have a good quality, one the audience can identify as human.

I'm not saying, either, that your antagonist has to be evil. In a romantic comedy, he shouldn't be. He should be a serious possibility when it comes to being a possible love object for one of the characters (see *Tin Cup* or *His Girl Friday*). In a sports movie, he's the opposition, though often less morally worthy of the goal than the protagonist, but he is not pure evil (*Bad News Bears*, *Rocky*). That would be too easy. Yes, we still must have a reason to consider him less worthy of winning, so he must have some evil characteristics. But he is a human being with all the wants and needs of a human being.

To Do

How do you draw a character like this? The same way you develop the protagonist. So ask yourself, do you know this character as well as you know your protagonist? Before you rewrite his role in your script, take the time now to write a character study in the same way you did for your protagonist. This time, pay special attention to elements that may explain why he went down the path to evil, if that's the kind of antagonist you have, or why he thinks he's fighting for what's his or what is right, according to him. Also, be careful to include a humanizing trait. Nobody is completely evil. Nobody is completely good. To be believable, your antagonist must ring true as a person.

REVEALING YOUR ANTAGONIST

Character is action. Action is character. When you read through your script (and you should read it through several times before undertaking your rewrite), look for places to show the character of your antagonist. Look for places to show how he interacts with people on a daily basis, how he interacts with his confederates or his family. Look for places to show his human side. And, especially, look for places to show his strengths and weaknesses, and, if necessary, his evil.

Just as the protagonist has a voice, so should the antagonist, assuming your antagonist is a person. Things to check for in the antagonist's dialogue: Is he too arch (over the top evil)? Does he sound human, or is he just a writer's two-dimensional conceit to move the story along?

Once you've read this character's dialogue completely through, compare and contrast his words with the protagonist's words. Make sure they're not speaking with the same voice. Their rhythms of speech should be distinct. Their vocabularies in contrast. Ensure that how they say something is as important as what they say.

For an excellent example of contrasting manners of speech, and a worthy opponent, look at Hans Gruber, the character played by Alan Rickman in *Die Hard* (screenplay by Jeb Stuart, based on the novel by Roderick Thorp). Here is an antagonist whose speech demonstrates his erudition and ruthlessness. He is able, in a critical moment, to imitate the speech of an American executive, thus showing his cunning. His manner of talking is a fundamental element of his character, just as fundamental as John McClane's (Bruce Willis) blue-collar, wise-cracking, no-nonsense speech.

But it isn't only his speech that he uses to deceive McClane, it is his cowering manner. He "acts" the victim to perfection, trying to gain McClane's confidence. Eventually, McClane gives him a pistol. Once he has his hands on the pistol, his whole demeanor changes, and he becomes Hans again. There's another reversal when he discovers the pistol is not loaded and that he hadn't fooled McClane after all. And yet another reversal when other members of his gang burst out of the elevator.

Definitely a worthy foe: ruthless, cunning, quick-witted, multi-lingual. Try and stop him!

McClane finally does, but he pays a price. It isn't easy, but the journey is worth it.

To Do
Write one line saying what your antagonist wants.

Chapter 4

Ensuring Dynamic Scenes

There is only one type of scene that should be in your movie: scenes that move the story forward and illuminate character. If a scene doesn't do one or both of these chores, then that scene doesn't belong in your screenplay. Once your scene passes that litmus test, what else do you need to know about your scene to make sure it's a good one?

Just as a good screenplay has a solid foundation in its structure, so does a scene. A scene has a beginning, a middle, and an end. It actually has all the seven points that a screenplay has, you just don't always see all the parts. Good writers come in as late as possible in the scripted scene and leave as soon as their point is made, but the scene as a whole has taken place on or off camera.

Look at *Shakespeare in Love* (written by Marc Norman and Tom Stoppard), one of the best screenplays of the last 25 years or so. A scene that exemplifies the seven-point structure comes near the middle of the story, when Viola, dressed as Thomas, returns to her home.

The ordinary life of the scene starts with a quick shot of her reading Shakespeare's love note to Viola and continues with Essex ranting in her chambers. When she enters as Viola, there is some small talk.

The inciting incident of the scene is when Essex announces that he has entered into a contract with her father for her hand in marriage. At this stage, Viola is still the protagonist of the scene, but that changes when she says she doesn't want the marriage to happen. Now it's Essex's turn to be the protagonist. He has a goal. He has come for something: to state his intentions to marry her and take her to Virginia. End of Act One of the scene.

The turning point of the scene is when he grabs and kisses her. She slaps him, turning the scene around and changing his attitude from solicitous (as solicitous as he can be, at least) to forceful and demanding.

At the low point, for Viola, he tells her how it's going to be with him in the Americas.

In the final challenge, he overcomes her objections by telling her the queen and her father have consented, meaning there's no way out. She capitulates.

There is no real return to normal life because the point has been made, time to move on. It's quite common to skip the first and last points in a scene, as they are often understood by the actions before and after them, and they do not need to be explained. Get in late and get out early.

Just as there are barriers (conflict) for the protagonist to overcome over the length of the film, so, too, there are smaller conflicts in each scene. In the beginning of a scene, somebody wants something. Somebody else either tries to prevent him from getting that, or wants something in opposition. The scene, then, is about the struggle. Learning what each one (or more) wants is the beginning of the scene. The struggle to get it is the middle. One or the other wins the struggle. That's the end of the scene. Somebody's got to win, somebody's got to lose. Even in a comedy. Especially in a comedy.

The central characteristic, the one element that every scene needs, is conflict. If there is no conflict, there is no scene.

To Do

Go through your beatsheet and examine each scene for conflict. Write what, exactly, is the conflict of each scene under your description of the scene. If there is no conflict, there is no scene. Sometimes you'll need to group several beats to make a whole scene, so not every beat will have conflict. For example, if you included an establishing shot of a beach, say, as a scene, but really it is just an establishing shot to show you're in Hawaii, group it with the next beat or beats and write what the conflict is for that group of beats.

What You Need and What You Don't

What if you've got a great scene that is really funny, or dramatic, or tear-jerking? If it doesn't move the story along its way, we don't need it. If we don't need it, we don't put it in. No matter how brilliant they are, only necessary scenes are allowed, no side trips to grandma's house, no stopping to smell the flowers along the way, no trips to the comedy store or theme park – unless they are essential for the story. Bad scenes that move the story forward can be fixed. Great scenes that don't move the story are irreparable. They slow down the movie (or the reader of your script) and tend to make an audience fidget or wonder "what the hell?"

To Do

Read through your beatsheet again (again!) and delete scenes that don't move the story forward or reveal character. If a scene doesn't have conflict, figure out what the conflict should be. If you can't find conflict in that scene, cut it. Be brutal!

I mean it.

How to Rewrite the Scene

As with everything else in writing, screen or otherwise, there are as many ways to write a scene as there are writers. That means good as well as bad. That means easy as well as difficult. That means I have some ideas on this subject, but they're not gospel; and to make things more complicated, I'm always changing them. But for now, here's how I suggest you do it when you do your rewrite.

I've already talked about the scene having a beginning, a middle, and an end. About it having conflict. Now let's talk about the course of that conflict and where we are in it when we enter and leave the scene, and why we're in it in the first place.

Every major player in a scene has an objective — he wants something. As Robin Swicord, screenwriter on *Little Women*, *The Perez Family*, and *Memoirs of a Geisha*, says, "I want. Everything comes from that." Usually, each character wants something different. Hence the conflict. We must also know what the emotion of that character is at the beginning of the scene, what his attitude is, and what his long-term goal is. There's a helluva difference between a scene that starts off with everyone pissed off at each other from the get go and one that starts with laughter. If you know your characters, you'll know what their emotions are at the beginning of the scene — are they happy, sad, angry — and what will happen to them during the scene. Unless they have cause to change (they may or may not), they should maintain that emotion throughout the scene. Actors look at scenes this way (or the good ones do), and they look for hints the writer has given them.

We also need to know what the subject and purpose of the scene is. Yes, it's to move the story forward, first and foremost. But it may also be to shed some light on a character, to reveal information, to provide an obstacle. Know what you want to get across with your scene.

AN ACTOR'S POV

According to Don Richardson, the late television director, when an actor looks at a scene, he looks at two key elements to guide him through the scene. One is feeling, the other is purpose. An actor looks at a scene and tries to discern what emotion he has at the beginning of the scene and if that emotion remains the same throughout the scene. It will only change if there is something to change it. He also looks at the character's goal throughout the scene. What is his objective?

So it's important to tell the actor what the objective/goal in the scene is and how he feels about it. We do this in a combination of dialogue and description (action). Character is action, action is conflict, conflict is drama. We learn who the character is by how he reacts to the conflict — the obstacles in the way of his achieving his goal.

How do we ensure that this will happen? By making sure there is an opposing force, whether it is the antagonist or simply another person or element which has an opposing goal. In *Platoon*, written by Oliver Stone, the NVR did not want to be captured. They evaded and sabotaged, taunted and hid from the platoon, frustrating them. When the platoon reaches the village looking for the NVR, the main obstacle is language and lack of willingness to cooperate. Conflict in every scene doesn't mean you have to have an argument, just that you have to have opposing goals. When you have opposing goals, characters test their mettle and show who they really are. In this scene, the soldiers get so angry trying to communicate and finding enemy supplies, they end up burning the village to the ground.

The basics are simple. Someone wants something; the other person doesn't want them to have it. In an action scene, that could translate to someone wanting to escape, but the other won't let him without a fight or a chase. Someone wants to kill the enemy, the other is the enemy that wants to kill back. Someone wants to rob a bank, others want to stop him. Someone wants to win a car race, someone else wants to win just as badly. Someone wants to destroy the Death Star, others want to destroy those pesky rebels. You get the idea. Much of the time the goal is forgotten midway through the action, but the action must be sustained by the con- flict — the opposition of the goals.

How does an individual action scene fit into the movie as a whole? And how does the central goal fit into the scene? Every scene must move the story forward. If it doesn't, it's out, no mat- ter how funny, how thrilling, how scary, how daring. The scene serves the story as a whole, except for the first sequence in a James Bond movie which rarely, if ever, has anything to do with the film as a whole. If the underwater fight between the Count of Monte Cristo and his jailer hadn't served the story, it would have been cut.

The scene needs to move the story. Therefore, part of the central goal must be accomplished in the scene. In *The Count of Monte Cristo* (written by Jay Wolpert, based on the novel by Alexandre Dumas), for example, the count must escape to have revenge. His goal in the underwater fight scene is to escape. He jumps off the cliff and takes the jailer with him. His goal is still to escape, but his more immediate goal is to get the keys so he can free himself from his chains. Once done, he drowns the jailer as part of his overall revenge. Now he is free to recreate himself and seek revenge on his accuser.

The short-term goal serves the long-term goal. The long- term goal drives the scene's necessity.

Overall, the most important element in the scene is the conflict that drives the action. The conflict is established by the obstacles that prevent the protagonist from reaching his goals.

Now where does your scene start? Okay, it starts at the beginning. No, it has a beginning, but it doesn't necessarily start in the beginning. It should, in fact, start as late into the scene as possible and end as soon as it has an ending (not necessarily at the end of the scene). What do I mean by this? Let's take a domestic fight, for example, say between Romeo and Juliet had they lived through that little misunderstanding about the poison. Romeo's got a dead-end job at a supermarket packing bags. Juliet's got a kid at her breast and one on the way. Romeo has been dressed down by the produce manager, and he's pissed.

Where do we start the argument over dinner not being ready (which is really an argument about him having to be a wage slave and her having no one to talk to all day)? We could start it when he slams the door on entry to their stifling one-bedroom, un-air conditioned hell hole in North Hollywood. We could start it when he sees her lying on the couch flipping channels with the remote. Or we could wait until he sits down at the table (not set for dinner) and starts pounding his fists. All, actually, good starting points depending on the ending point you have in mind. I vote for the fists banging on the table, but there's no set place to begin this scene. It all depends on what you want to say.

Where do we end this revelation of domestic bliss that confronts teenagers who get married on impulse? If we had started it when the door slammed, we could have ended it at the fists hitting the table. If we start it at the fists hitting the table, we can end it when he throws the dish of spaghetti (again!) to the floor, or when he clips her one, or when he stomps out the door. You decide. It depends on what you want to say about Romeo and Juliet, where you are in the movie, what their emotions are, where you started the scene in the first place. I'd end it before he left the house — we've seen that, and we know he's going to do that. But that's me. I like shorthand in my movies.

To Do

One more time through the beatsheet, this time to note what the protagonist of the scene (which could be anyone, not necessarily the protagonist of your movie) wants. What is his emotion at the start of the scene? And what is the purpose of the scene?

Just in case I haven't mentioned it sufficiently, let me underline it again: *The element most new (and many experienced) screenwriters leave out of their scenes is conflict.* Without conflict, there is no drama. Without drama (even in a comedy), there is no story. Without conflict, there is no movement. No change. Conflict is the key element of the scene.

THE SEQUENCE

Sometimes it's easier to think of a movie in terms of the main sequences. A sequence is a group of scenes that all have a common flow and purpose. They might take place over a period of time and in several locations, but they have a thematic unity. And, of course, they have filmic structure, which is to say, they have a seven-point structure as well.

Often sequences are found at important story points. In *Thelma & Louise*, for example, there is a fine sequence that makes up the inciting incident and another that forms the midpoint of the movie. If you haven't seen this movie in a few years, go rent it and watch carefully. It's a superbly constructed film. Its midpoint sequence, for example, focuses on Thelma's midpoint change, though it cross cuts with Louise and her boyfriend.

The ordinary life of that sequence is the scene where Louise gives Thelma the money that Jimmy, Louise's boyfriend, has brought her.

The inciting incident of the sequence is when J.D. comes to Thelma's door, all wet and seductive. Thelma takes him in and her life changes. Darryl and she had been together since she was fourteen. He was the only man she ever knew. Now she learns a thing or two about sex with J.D.

The end of Act One of the sequence is when J. D. takes Thelma's wedding ring and dumps it in a glass. At this stage, he's the protagonist. He's driving the action. He has a plan.

The midpoint of the sequence is when Thelma shows up the next morning in the coffee shop light headed and drunk with sex. That is, until Louise asks her where the money is.

The low point is the discovery that J. D. has stolen it. Now the story spins off in a new direction because this is the low point of the midpoint (confused yet?). Thelma wants to maintain that "It's okay," but Louise says, "It's not okay. None of this is okay."

The final challenge of the sequence is when Thelma takes charge and gets Louise packed and into the car.

The return to normal life for the sequence is when they take off in the car, resuming their life on the road.

To Do

Now, review your beatsheet once again (see how handy they are?) and group your scenes into sequences that make sense. Some rearranging might be in order, and not all scenes will fit into a sequence. That's all right. Now it's time to rewrite the scenes keeping in mind all that you've learned up to this point:

The scene must have a purpose. It must have a protagonist and an antagonist. It must have conflict. It has a seven-point structure, though it could start late and end early. It may be part of a sequence with its own seven points.

At this stage, you can do the exercise or you can wait until we've discussed description and dialogue. I'd do the exercise.

CHAPTER 5

MAKING
DESCRIPTIONS
LEAP OFF
THE PAGE

Here's one of the basic contradictions a writer has to face. You know that a reader, probably not the producer, is going to be the first person at the production company or studio to read your script, so you have to impress this person. (A reader is someone an executive, agent, or producer hires to read a script and write a report that includes an analysis, a summary, and a recommendation. A reader is the first person empowered to say no to your work. And she usually does because that's the safest thing to do.) We know that motion pictures are all about what you see on screen, so you'd think that the descriptive passages of a script would be important. And they are. But readers often skip through them to get to the dialogue because they think, sometimes correctly, that the character is shaped by the dialogue. And dialogue is easier to read. But harder to write.

So does that mean you shouldn't pay attention to description? No. Does it mean that you shouldn't write visually? No, on the contrary. You should still make the reader see the movie as best you can, and that's where your writing style for descriptive paragraphs will pay off.

Before you start to rewrite all the descriptions in your script, let's talk a little about what your pages should look like and why.

First of all, pity the poor script readers. They generally read two, sometimes three, scripts per day. Their eyes get tired. They need white space to rest them on. If your script reduces their eye fatigue, they will automatically be happier with your script. So you want to make their job easier by giving them lots of white space.

No, you will not sell a script based on the amount of white space on a page. But you may lose the reader's interest if he or she has to plow through dense and long paragraphs. So, you want to make your paragraphs as short and succinct as possible. Michael Goldenberg, who wrote the screenplay for *Contact* and *Peter Pan* and is writing the screenplay for the fifth *Harry Potter* film, says you want to make your description "efficient but provocative." Jack Epps, Jr., who co-wrote *Top Gun*, *Legal Eagles*, and *Dick Tracy*, urges writers to "write in small fragments using verbs instead of nouns."

No one has ever been accused of having too little description. Screenplays are terse, filled with short phrases emphasizing verbs always — *always* — in the present tense.

```
Connor drags himself to the bed. Falls.
Checks his arm. Blood spurts out of
his wrist. He slams his other palm on
it. Nearly faints.
```

Short declarative sentences. Fragments. Lots of verbs. But the scene is clear as a bell, isn't it? You can *see* it, can't you? You don't need to know what kind of bed it is, or even what Connor looks like. You see the action, and that's what counts. Let the make-up artist, the set designer, the production designer, the wardrobe designer, the director of photography, and the director fill in the rest. Let them do their jobs. Your job is to make them see the film, see the action, and move on.

But what would Mrs. Thrall, your tenth grade English teacher, say about using fragments (not to mention starting a sentence with a conjunction)? I don't care what she would say. (Though, believe me, I respect her and all she taught me.) This is screenwriting, not a critical analysis of *Moby Dick*. You don't have to follow the conventions of English usage, but you do have to use English in a way that gets people excited about your story. So you use whatever works.

On the other hand, you can't sound like you don't know how to use the conventions of modern English. You have to know the rules to break the rules. So you must be correct in subject/verb agreement, use of your/you're, their/there/they're, and such confusing things as the difference between lay and lie (if you don't know, look it up, it'll stay with you longer). That means spelling and punctuation, too, though you can certainly bend the rules with punctuation. You don't want readers to misjudge your screenplay because it has grammatical mistakes where it shouldn't. Making mistakes on purpose is one thing. Making them because of laziness or ignorance is another.

How will the reader know the difference? She will, believe me. Just like you can spot sloppy production values like a mike hanging in a scene, unless that's done on purpose in a "mocumentary."

USING SUBTEXT TO UNDERSCORE YOUR MEANING

Subtext is the meaning under the words or actions. Words and actions can have apparent meaning and, in so doing, serve the story. But they can also have meaning below the text, meaning not directly spelled out, that can also serve the story. Why do we care about subtext? Because anything that can make a movie richer, that can give it more depth, texture, complexity, is a good thing. It will reach people on more than one level and give them a deeper appreciation of what you're trying to get across. Especially if you do it in action.

Let's look at *To Kill a Mockingbird* for subtext. The scene with the rabid dog is a good example of subtext in physical action. We know that Atticus (the Gregory Peck character) is a peacemaker, yet we are surprised to learn that he's such a good shot, the sheriff gives him a rifle to shoot the rabid dog with. It's a surprise even to his children that he's the "best shot in town." What are we to make of this, and why do we need it since it's not about the main course of action?

It tells us that Atticus *chooses* to be a peacemaker. He has the ability to defend himself and children if he wants to, but he chooses words instead of bullets to do so. This will come to play later when he's confronted on the jailhouse steps by the mob. He could have brought a rifle, assuming he owned one, but he brought only his words. Just as he warned Scout not to fight no matter what anyone says, he never stoops to violence or anger when attacked verbally, or even when he's spit on. More character.

Of course, there is always the knowledge, running below the text, that he could choose differently. It may even be inferred (here's another pair of words to look up — infer and imply) that he spent time in the army. That creates a tension of its own — will he use his skills when the children are in danger?

How Long Is a Paragraph?
Short.

As short as one word. Maybe two. Just like a sentence. Whatever it takes to give your words kick. An impact. Play fast and loose with what Mrs. Thrall taught you (I can see her spinning in her grave now). You don't need a subject sentence with several sentences supporting it. All you need is the action. A rule of thumb (a short thumb) is to keep paragraphs under four lines. If you have a longer need, break the paragraphs up into shots — visualize the scene. How would the director cut it? Describe each shot briefly and move on.

That's visual storytelling.

That's what works in a screenplay.

Read the following excerpt from the screenplay for a children's movie and see if you can visualize the individual shots.

FADE IN:

EXT. SOCCER FIELD - DAY

A ball flies past a 13-year-old GOALIE and into the net.

                    CARLOS
          Gooooaaaaal!

Then...

CARLOS RANDALL

11, shaggy, straight black hair, baggy soccer uniform. He is not on the field but standing with a group of other TEAM MEMBERS, all bigger than he is, YELLING ad lib encouragement to their TEAMMATE who has just scored.

Groups of SPECTATORS watch and cheer. Among them,

AMANDA,

Carlos' mother, 30s, dark, sunken eyes that have seen some pain. Carlos' TEAMMATES and OP-PONENTS reposition themselves on the field.

The furor dies down, and Carlos and a few other boys sit down on the bench again.

The COACH, balding, squat, but tightly muscled, makes a T with his hands and...

```
          COACH
     Time out!

A WHISTLE blows and the game stops.

          COACH
     Chen and Williams, go
     in for Charles and
     Stein. Go go go...

The TWO KIDS race onto the field. They run to
their teammates...

          CARLOS
     Coach! What about me?
     I'm ready.

          COACH
     I know you are,
     Carlos. Hang on. Soon.

Carlos turns away, disappointed, as the TWO
KIDS who were playing trot off the field to the
bench and take their seats next to him.
```

SOME OTHER RULES

Screenplays are always written in the present tense to give you a sense of immediacy. It's happening right now, right here. On the screen.

That also means you only write what you see on screen. You can't write the characters' histories (background) because the viewer (as opposed to the reader) won't see that on screen. You can't write inner thoughts. You can't write emotions that aren't played out. You can't write plans or hidden desires. You can only write what the viewer will see. That means you have to find a way to express all of that in action and dialogue.

To Do

Go through the descriptive paragraphs in your screenplay and see if you can take out all the adverbs and as many adjectives and nouns as possible. Shorten your sentences. Shorten your paragraphs.

THE WAY THEY USED TO DO IT

In the heyday of the silent film, the only way to get your point across in a scene was to *show* it. Sure, there were title cards, but the story was developed with actions and images. The actors developed a style to express emotion, and words weren't needed. With the advent of sound, film acting became more subtle. A minute change in a facial expression could cause or be caused by a word or line of dialogue.

Still, today, even with completely naturalistic sound and lighting, the most effective way to tell your story is with actions and images. They're universal. They're not lost in translation in the foreign market.

Sure, it seems more efficient to just tell the audience what you want them to know by putting the information in dialogue. But nothing is more boring than sitting through five minutes of verbal exposition. Especially if you can *show* it in one simple image. What's more effective, showing the Death Star rotating in space or Luke Skywalker saying, "Look, there's a huge man-made planet that looks impenetrable"?

Okay, that's the easy stuff. How do you show a character's background or thoughts? Sometimes you *will* have to resort to dialogue, but it's better if you don't. What if you want to tell us that he grew up on a ranch? Try describing worn cowboy boots, a way of walking, and maybe even a little bit of "chaw" in his cheek. What if you want to show he's angry? He spits a bit of the chaw in an inappropriate place. What if you want us to know he's planning to compete in the rodeo today? He practices with a lariat.

All pretty easy, I admit. I chose my examples carefully, but look to the *behavior* of your character to tell the story. Write description an actor can play. Yes, you can say he's angry because he can play angry, but it's even more effective to the reader if he charges into the bunkhouse, tips over a bunk bed and kicks it to splinters.

Just about any emotion can be played by an actor, especially if you give him some actions to work with. Thoughts and plans are much harder, so you will have to find a way to externalize them or put them into dialogue. Building models, unfolding plans, surveying a plot of land (not literally, just looking it over), or even just picking up a travel brochure can say a lot about your story. Maybe not everything, but a lot. Have your people *do*, not talk.

To Do

Find a scene that is heavy in dialogue and try to express it completely in action and description. I said try. It may not be possible, but in the fifty or so classes I've used this exercise, it's produced hundreds of superior scenes relying on images and actions alone.

When you've finished that scene, go through your whole movie and apply what you've learned in this chapter to your descriptive paragraphs. Make them short. Punchy. Verb heavy. Use them as substitutes for dialogue whenever possible so that your pages aren't "too dense."

CHAPTER 6

LIFE SUPPORT FOR YOUR PROTAGONIST

Let's talk about supporting players. If your story has only a protagonist and an antagonist, it's going to be pretty thin. They need
friends, colleagues, allies in their battle. And the old adage, "You're
known by the company you keep," is very true in film. It's one
way we learn who the central character is — by the people he
surrounds himself with. So, are your supporting characters doing
all they can do to support your protagonist and the story?

Let's look at *The Wizard of Oz*, that veritable textbook
of screenwriting. Not only do the supporting characters help
Dorothy in her quest to return home, they also represent parts

of Dorothy's personality, as Chris Vogler has pointed out in his essential book, *The Writer's Journey*. That is, they represent parts of her personality that need development. The cowardly lion helps Dorothy to face things the way they are and not run away from them — a lesson he must learn, too. The tin man underscores Dorothy's need for empathy with others. The straw man represents her need to use her own wits instead of always relying on her aunt and uncle to get her out of scrapes. Even the good witch stands for something inside Dorothy — her innate goodness and love of her home and family. She just needs a little reminding that there's no place like home.

Each of these characters has his own arc. Each shows us who he is by what he does and says. Each seeks to be validated for the trait he most admires, and each displays that trait and receives an award from the Wizard to prove he has it. And Dorothy, by the time she reaches the Wizard, has proven she has all three traits.

In *The Green Mile* (screenplay by Frank Darabont based on the novel by Stephen King), many of the supporting players are there to contrast with Paul as a way of bringing out his character, which, though upright and respectable, is somewhat drab. In one sequence in the film, we see all kinds of behavior and dialogue that sets up Paul (the character played by Tom Hanks) and shows him to be a compassionate man despite the fact that he supervises the warehousing, and then execution, of prisoners. The people around him are interesting in themselves, and create interest in the movie for the viewer.

Around scene 33 of the shooting script, Toot, a trusty played by Michael Jeter, begins the rehearsal of an upcoming execution of a Native American. We learn just who he is in a pair of lines: "Sittin' down, sittin' down, rehearsing now! Everybody settle!" He's comfortable enough with his keeper to feel free to mimic him irreverently. His repetitive speech tells us that he may be missing a few marbles. He makes us laugh in the midst of what should be supremely solemn. And, eventually, he gives Paul the opportunity to point that out, as he does at the end of scene 51 (when he talks about trying not to laugh in church). So Paul, by contrast, is a compassionate, serious person with respect for human dignity.

In this sequence Darabont also further sets up Percy's (Don Hutchison) evil when we see he learns about the wetting of the sponge. Later, his brutal act (not to be confused with the respectable Brutal, the David Morse character) further underlines Paul's innate goodness. We've suspected Percy for some time, and have been wondering since the previous scene how his evil is going to manifest itself. Soon we'll know. If Percy is evil, Paul is good.

During the final part of the rehearsal, Paul's compassion and tolerance of Toot is underscored with a roll of his eyes and a choice to ignore the intruding mouse. Contrast this with Percy's behavior in the previous sequence when the mouse outruns him and his traps.

Paul is one determined and compassionate man. How do we know? By how he reacts to the supporting characters, and by how they stand in stark contrast to him.

So what do your supporting characters support? Are they sounding boards for your central character? Are they contrasts? Are they really facets of the central character, as in *The Wizard of Oz*, there to help her grow and become the woman she needs to be?

To Do

Make sure each supporting character has a purpose and that you know what that purpose is. List each supporting character of importance (you don't need to write down characters such as POLICE OFFICER 2) and what his purpose in the script is. If you don't know why he's there, cut or replace him with somebody who has purpose.

DEVELOPING THEIR PERSONALITIES

Now you have all the supporting characters that you need, but they just seem to stand there like pillars, holding up their end of the bargain. Nothing special. Okay, maybe one or two are special. But how do you make them stand out? How do you separate your supporting characters from the people that just come and go in your protagonist's life?

The easy way? Give them a quirk: something unusual about their dress code, their speech (either how they speak or what they talk about), even the way they use their hands. This allows you to paint a picture of a character in very few words, while still giving their appearance the impact that you want. Part of that impact is how the supporting character sets off your protagonist. Look at *Beverly Hills Cop* (story by Danilo Bach and Daniel Petrie, Jr., screenplay by Daniel Petrie, Jr.). I still remember the boutique barista, Serge, played by Bronson Pinchot, for his accent, dialogue, and mannerisms. He's one small character who served as a foil for Eddie Murphy in that scene, but he stands out from the crowd. He helped increase the comedy in that film, always a good thing (if intentional).

Okay, how about a supporting player with a much more important role? Think of the breakthrough role for Brad Pitt in *Thelma & Louise*. As J. D., he stood out because of his cowboy hat, his clothes, and his six pack, not to mention that slow, seductive drawl. We didn't have to be with him for a minute before we knew what went on inside his head and what his motives were. He had several appearances in the film, and they all had a function. He was essential for Thelma's sexual revolution. The skills he taught her regarding hold-ups were job training which lead to an escalation of the action after the midpoint. He served a very definite set of functions and helped the central character develop so the story could charge on. Did he change? Probably not. But he didn't have to.

Not all supporting characters have to have their own arc. In the best of movies, many of them do, but not all. In action movies, few do, and it doesn't matter. Often, even the protagonist doesn't change. (Isn't Bond still Bond after all these years? Okay, the new Bond is vulnerable, but he soon reverts to form.)

One supporting character who was essential was Han Solo in *Star Wars*, written by George Lucas. He's a hardboiled space jockey who's in it for the money. But as Leia tells him, if he's in it only for the money, that's all he'll get. We see him slowly change from a mercenary to a mentor to a hero in the course of the film.

So what should you be doing to make sure that your supporting characters are not only doing their job, but making an impression? Yes, a movie is about the protagonist's struggle, but it's also about his world and the people in it. So let's make those people stand out in the service of the story.

To Do

Go through your story and identify the supporting characters who are most important. Beef up their screen presence by giving them a quirk of some sort. Make them stand out. Have the quirk relate to their personality or function regarding your protagonist or your antagonist.

CHAPTER 7

PARING
IT
DOWN

I can absolutely guarantee you, based on more than twenty years experience, that the second thing a reader (be she a reader, development exec, agent, producer, or studio head) will do when she gets your script, is thumb through to the end to see what the page count is. The first, of course, is to read the title and name, possibly your agent's name and contact info. But the most important issue for her will be the length.

What? Length over quality? You mean to tell me you'll be judged on length? Not exactly. Here's how it works. Readers read two or three scripts a day. A long one makes the day long. It will be read later in the day or put off until tomorrow. When tomorrow comes, it will be read later in the day or put off until the next day. Wouldn't you do that?

Development execs, producers, and studio executives know that audiences will sit for 90 minutes to two hours to watch a film. Distributors and exhibitors like films that length because you can fit more showings in a day than with a three-hour film. More showings, more money. So which script would they like to read first, the 100-page script or the 150-page script? Yes, I know, *The Green Mile* was 185 pages. But you're not Frank Darabont, and neither am I. They're gonna look at the page count.

And that page count will influence their attitude when they begin reading. They can't help it. So you want to make them eager to read your work, not dread it. Ideally, then, you want your script to come in under 120 pages, preferably closer to 110. Some genres should even be shorter — I wrote films for children that needed to be in the low 80s. A good comedy might be 95. An epic might be a little longer, but unless you're Oliver Stone, I'd keep it short. If you find yourself edging over 120, it's time to take a serious look at how to lose a little weight. As a matter of fact, I've never read a first draft that wouldn't be improved by taking 10% off of it. Even though you've polished and shaped, and the diamond is clear and all facets are shining, you could still take a little off the top and sides (to mix metaphors).

THE FIRST STEP TO PAGE REDUCTION

Cut out all carbohydrates. No, sorry, that's the diet you'll have to go on after you finish this draft because you will have gained so much weight from being cooped up behind your computer for months on end. The first thing you'll need to do is go back to your beatsheet and look over the beats. Does every single one of them move the story forward or reveal something crucial about your protagonist? Preferably, each beat does both. If not, try to combine some scenes. If a scene does neither, cut it. Be ruthless. If you're not sure, take the scene out for a moment, read the scene before and the scene after without the scene in question. Do you lose anything? Does the story still make sense? Then leave it out. If you can get by with just a little additional work in the preceding or following scene, then do that. If there's no way in hell your movie can move forward without that scene, then leave it in.

Michael Goldenberg says, "Cutting is the most powerful tool you have." Use it.

To Do
Cut 10% of the scenes in your movie by combining them, adjusting them, or cutting them altogether.

CUTTING DOWN SCENES

This is getting bloody, but soon it's going to go to the bone, so take a deep breath. Let's say that what remains after the slaughter of the 10% are scenes crucial to the storytelling of your movie. Fine. Now let's cut down each individual scene by 10%. How to do that? Remember when we were talking about the structure of scenes and we said that it's a good idea to enter as late as possible and leave as soon as you've accomplished your goal for the scene? You can enter even later and leave even earlier.

First of all, sometimes it's not necessary to show the ordinary life segment of the scene, especially if we've been in this place or with these people before. We already know what their ordinary life is going to be. So you may, so long as it's not confusing, start with what the Spanish call the *detonante* of the scene. The detonator. We call it the inciting incident. It's what kicks off the action of the scene and propels it. It's what makes the need of the protagonist of the scene come alive.

In some cases, you can start even after that, so long as we understand what that need is and what the protagonist's drive is by inferring something from the previous scene.

In the middle of the scene, you can cut down on description, especially specifics as to the decoration of a room, the foliage of an outdoor place, or whatever gets in the way of the forward action. Certainly take out any camera direction and placement. That's not for you to determine anyway, and it only gets in the way of the reading. Let the director do the job. All you want to do is to enable the reader to visualize the story, not every single shot.

As you approach the end of your scene, try to determine when you've made the point of the scene, and cut out everything that follows that point. That probably will mean you can cut the return to normal life at the end of the scene. You can sometimes even cut the final challenge of the scene if we can predict the outcome from what we've learned about the characters or from what we're about to see in the next scene.

For example, let's say that you've established that the quiet, self-effacing character played by Jackie Chan will do everything in his power not to fight an enemy, unless provoked by a reference to his mother. And let's say the scene leads up to that. Do we really need to see the fight? Well, yes and no. It's a Jackie Chan movie, so, yes, it's all about the fight. However, let's say a not-so-elegant actor is playing the role and it's not a martial arts movie, then we could cut from the challenge to the next scene where he's walking down the street carrying the pistols the other character brandished. We get the picture.

To Do

Choose a ten-page excerpt from your script that you think is pretty tight already. Now cut a page from it. Use any tricks you can think of, but get it down to nine pages.

You see, it was possible.

CUTTING DIALOGUE

How do you cut dialogue without cutting information that is essential to the story? First of all, you make sure that you absolutely must have that information in dialogue. It's probably more effective to see in action. Action is quicker. They're called *motion* pictures, and if you can move your story forward with moving pictures only, you'll make more of an impression on your audience that if you rely entirely on words (dialogue). If you illuminate your character by a physical attribute or something he does, it's always going to be better than having you tell about it in dialogue.

Then, assuming you've changed any dialogue to action that you could, are all the remaining words necessary? Quite often, you'll find that characters go through a little "throat clearing" at the beginning of their speeches. Sometimes, that can be good as a trait of your character. But mostly it's not. It's a waste of reader's time, just like, "Hello. How are you?" would be. Or even a "Goodbye" on the telephone. If they waste time, if they're not absolutely needed, then they're out.

Then you'll need to make sure each word of dialogue is authentic to that character. Would he really say those lines, those words? Would a street tough call a rival "effete"?

While you're doing this, you can make sure the dialogue conveys character. That means we can learn something from the way he says something as much as from what he says. For example, what's the difference between "busy as hell" and "busier than a one-armed paper hanger"?

One last question. Could another character have said that sentence? If so, then it's probably not in character. That means you'll either have to change the language to suit the character or re-assign the line to another.

Then there's dialogue that's unnecessary because you've already told the reader or the audience that information in another way. Often, you'll have one character tell another character something he doesn't know, but that the reader knows because she's read it earlier. In that case, cut deeper into the scene. Sometimes you'll write something in description that a character then describes in dialogue. Cut one or the other. Preferably the dialogue.

To Do

Read the following pages. Cut them from twenty pages to twelve pages by eliminating wasteful, repetitious, or character-inappropriate dialogue. Cut descriptive lines that aren't needed or don't move the action. Be brutal. This scene definitely needs help!

FADE IN:

INT. R & J'S APARTMENT - EVENING

We can hear the wail of an infant who wants
her dinner. We can also hear the grunts and
groans and the moans and heavy breathing of a
pair of people having sex. As the camera tours
the living room, we can see what a shambles
it's in, with clothing strewn everywhere,
dirty dishes on top of dirty dishes on top of
newspapers and magazines. The television is on
in the corner. The windows have baby handprints
on them. The floor is a mess.

We follow the moans and groans to one of the
bedrooms and find JULIET, 19, pretty, long,
dark hair, receiving VICENTE, 21. They're
enjoying this a lot, but Juliet's concerned.
She's afraid Romeo's going to be coming home
soon and she wants Vicente out as soon as
possible. She's putting everything she can
into the effort to finish quickly.

           JULIET
      Yes, yes. Come on,
      Javvie. Come on, boy.

          VICENTE
    (breathing hard, he's
    thinking she really likes
    him)

                    VICENTE (CONT'D)
          Juliet, Juliet, I...
          I... I love you. I'm
          going to... I'm going
          to...

LOUD DOOR KNOCKS

Vicente suddenly stops. He looks towards the
door.

                    VICENTE
          What's that?

                    ROMEO (OS)
          Julie! Come on. Open
          up. I'm hungry.

                    JULIET
          Oh, no. It's my
          husband! Hurry up! You
          have to go.

                    VICENTE
          I'm almost finished.

She pushes him off and jumps out of bed. She
dresses quickly as she talks. He just sits there
at first trying to figure out what happened. She
tells him to get moving.

                    JULIET
          You are finished.
          We're both finished if
          you don't get out of

JULIET (CONT'D)
here. Hurry up and get
dressed. I'll stall
him while you go out
the window.

VICENTE
What? It's two stories
down, girl. What am I,
Superman?

JULIET
You said you were a
couple of minutes ago.

VICENTE
And that was like,
that was like what I
felt, but, like I
said, it was really
that I meant you make
me feel like Superman.
Why can't you stay a
little while longer?

JULIET
Because Romeo will be
pissed off that his
dinner's not on the
table and that little
Romeo's crying.

VICENTE
Why don't you let me
talk to him to see if--

>   JULIET
>   Are you out of your
>   mind? Get out of here,
>   now. Take the fire
>   escape. Hurry up
>   before he bursts in
>   here.

>   VICENTE
>   Okay, if you're so
>   worried. I'll do it.

He gets up to hug her but she's already dressed
and goes out into the hallway, shutting the
door behind her.

INT. R & J'S APARTMENT - EVENING

The knocking continues on the door as Juliet
walks through the messy living room. She goes
to the door, which had a chain on it and a
deadbolt.

>   JULIET
>   Who is it?

>   ROMEO (OS)
>   (through the door)
>   Julie, who the hell do
>   you think it is? It's
>   your husband home for
>   dinner, and it had
>   better be good. Open
>   the damn door. What's
>   the matter with you?

She unlocks the door, undoes the chain, and
ROMEO, 20, storms in. He's wearing black
pants, a white shirt with a loosened black
tie, and a green apron. He has a name tag on
his shirt that says, "I'm Romeo. Ask me about
the produce here."

                ROMEO
          Jeez, what a sty. What
          have you been doing
          all day?
          (on hearing baby
          Romeo crying)
          Is that the baby? What
          the hell's going on
          here? Why did you have
          the door locked like
          that?

                JULIET
          There have been some
          break-ins. I didn't
          feel safe.

There's a crash that sounds like it came from
the bedroom.

                ROMEO
          What the...

He runs down the hall and into the

INT. R & J'S APARTMENT (BEDROOM) - EVENING

Romeo enters running and finds baby Romeo crawling on his hands and knees, a lamp broken into little pieces lying on the floor.

> ROMEO
> Juliet! Get your sorry
> ass in here.

> JULIET
> Romeo, I can explain.
> It's just that I've
> been so lone--

But she stops as she enters the room and sees it's just baby Romeo and the lamp. She also notices that the bed has been made and the window to the fire escape is still open, the curtain flowing in the breeze.

> ROMEO
> You've been what?

> JULIET
> I've been lonesome
> without you, honey.

She tries to throw her arms around his neck, but he won't have any of it.

> ROMEO
> (angry)
> Clean this mess up,
> will you, before Baby

> ROMEO (CONT'D)
> Romy gets hurt. I'm
> going to take a
> shower. I had to work
> in the parking lot
> half the day. And I
> get home and the house
> is a mess, the kid is
> out of control, and
> there's no food.
> Dinner better be on
> the table when I get
> out.

INT. R & J'S APARTMENT (KITCHEN)- EVENING

It's a small kitchen with a little table near a
window. There are two chairs at the table and a
high chair for the kid. Juliet is stirring pots
while the baby is sitting in his high chair and
eating applesauce. Or moving it around from one
place on his tray to another. We can hear the
television on in the other room. It's some sort
of news program talking about rising house
costs.

> JULIET
> (yelling)
> Did you get that
> raise?

> ROMEO (OS)
> (yelling)
> No. The sons of

                    ROMEO (CONT'D)
          bitches gave it to
          Herbie. He's such a
          suck up. If I had
          sucked up as much as
          he has, I'd be using
          Charmin to clean the
          brown off my nose.

                    JULIET
                  (yelling)
          But you'd be making
          two dollars an hour
          more and we'd be able
          to get another place.

                    ROMEO(OS)
                  (yelling)
          Shut up! I'm in no
          mood.

Juliet throws a couple of plates down on the
counter, pulls a colander out of the sink,
dumps some just boiled spaghetti onto the
plates, drops the colander back in the sink,
then grabs a sauce pan and ladles out some
red sauce on the spaghetti.

                    JULIET
                  (yelling)
          Dinner!

Romeo walks in, wearing a nice pair of pants
and a clean shirt. He looks like he's ready
to go somewhere.

JULIET
You going somewhere?

ROMEO
I'm gonna have a beer
with the guys.

JULIET
You're going out? I
thought we could spend
some time together
tonight.

ROMEO
Hey, I worked my ass
off today. I deserve a
little time off from
the grind. If you
fixed up the place a
little and took a
shower every once in a
while, maybe I'd stay
here.

JULIET
What, you think I'm
playing Wheel of
Fortune here all day?
It's hard work taking
care of the kid and
this dump while you're
off talking to people
and making eyes at the
girls and sneaking
drinks and stuff to
your homeboys.

Romeo kisses baby Romeo on the top of his
head, then sits down. He takes up his cutlery
and starts banging them on the table.

> JULIET
> What's the matter with
> you, I'm coming.

> ROMEO
> I said I wanted dinner
> on the table.

> JULIET
> I want a lot of things
> and I don't seem to be
> getting them either.

She slams a dish of the spaghetti on the table. He takes one look at and...

> ROMEO
> Spaghetti, again!

He flips the plate onto the floor. Juliet looks
at him.

> JULIET
> Are you crazy?

> ROMEO
> No, just hungry.
> Hungry and tired of
> your bullshit.

He storms out of the room. Baby Romy starts
to cry.

              JULIET
      Where are you going?

              ROMEO
      To get what I need for
      a change.

              JULIET
      What about me?

              ROMEO
      Aren't you already
      getting what you need
      from Vicente!

The door slams in the living room and Juliet
looks down at the pile of broken plate and
spaghetti on the floor. She shakes her head.
She comforts Baby Romeo.

              JULIET
      Don't worry, Romy.
      This ain't gonna
      happen again.

Now, before you read on, do the exercise. Best way to do this is to photocopy these pages (and these pages only, of course), then mark them up. Then come back here to see another way to do it.

Okay, it was tough, right? But not impossible. Here's how I might do it:

FADE IN:

INT. R & J'S APARTMENT - EVENING

An infant WAILS.

GRUNTS and GROANS of people having sex.

The living room is in a shambles - clothing
strewn everywhere, dirty dishes on top of newspapers and magazines.

IN THE BEDROOM

JULIET, 19, long, dark hair, receives VICENTE,
21. Juliet's putting everything she can into
the effort.

    JULIET
   Yes, yes. Come on,
   Javvie. Come on,
   boy.

    VICENTE
   Juliet, Juliet,
   I... I... I love
   you. I'm going to...
   I'm going to...

LOUD DOOR KNOCKS

Vicente suddenly stops. He looks towards the
door.

                    VICENTE
          What's that?

                    JULIET
          Oh, no. It's Romeo.
          You have to get
          out of here.

                    VICENTE
          I'm almost finished.

She pushes him off, jumps out of bed.

                    JULIET
          You are finished.

She dresses quickly.

                    JULIET
          We're both finished
          if you don't get
          out of here. Hurry
          up and get dressed.
          I'll stall him while
          you go out the window.

                    VICENTE
          What? It's two stories
          down, girl. What am I,
          Superman?

                    JULIET
          You said you were a
          couple of minutes
          ago.

                    VICENTE
          I meant, like, you
          make me feel like
          Superman, you know?
          Why don't you let
          me talk to him.
          See if--

                    JULIET
          Are you out of your
          mind? Get out of here.
          Take the fire escape.
          Hurry!

He gets up to hug her, but she's already moving
out of the room. She shuts the door behind her.

INT. R & J'S APARTMENT - EVENING

The knocking continues. Juliet reaches the
door which has a deadbolt and chain.

                    JULIET
          Who is it?

                    ROMEO (O.S.)
          (through the door)
               Who the hell do
               you think it is?
               Open the damn door.

She unlocks the door, undoes the chain, and
ROMEO, 20, storms in. He wears black pants, a
white shirt with a loosened black tie, and a
green apron. His name tag says, "I'm Romeo.
Ask me about the produce here."

The baby CRIES.

>   ROMEO
> What the hell's
> going on here? Why
> did you have the
> door locked like
> that?

>   JULIET
> There have been
> some break-ins. I
> didn't feel safe.

There's a crash that sounds like it came from
the bedroom.

>   ROMEO
>   What the...

He runs down the hall and into

THE BEDROOM.

Romeo enters running and finds baby Romeo
crawling on his hands and knees, a lamp broken
into little pieces lying on the floor.

>   ROMEO
> Juliet! Get your
> sorry ass in here.

>   JULIET (O.S.)
> Romeo, I can explain.
> It's just that I've
> been so lone--

But she stops as she enters the room and sees
it's just baby Romeo and the lamp. The bed has
been made and the window to the fire escape is
still open.

                    ROMEO
          You been what?

                    JULIET
          I've been lonesome
          without you, honey.

She tries to throw her arms around his neck,
but he won't have any of it.

                    ROMEO
            (angry)
          Clean this shit up
          before Baby Romy
          gets hurt. I'm going
          to take a shower.
          Dinner better be on
          the table when I get
          out.

INT. R & J'S APARTMENT (KITCHEN) - EVENING

It's a small kitchen with a little table near
a window. There are two chairs and a high
chair at the table.

Juliet cooks while the baby sits in his high
chair moving applesauce from one place on his
tray to another. The television blasts in the
other room.

                    JULIET
                 (yelling)
              Did you get that
              raise?

                    ROMEO (O.S.)
                 (yelling)
              No. The sons of
              bitches gave it to
              Herbie. If I had
              sucked up as much
              as he has, I'd be
              using Charmin to
              blow my nose.

                    JULIET
                 (yelling)
              But you'd be making
              two dollars an hour
              more, and we'd be
              able to get another
              place.

                    ROMEO (O.S.)
              Shut up! I'm in no
              mood.

Juliet throws a couple of plates down on the
counter, pulls a colander out of the sink,
dumps some spaghetti onto the plates, drops the
colander back in the sink, grabs a sauce pan,
ladles out some red sauce on the spaghetti.

              JULIET
            (yelling)
          Dinner!

Romeo walks in, wearing a nice pair of pants
and a clean shirt.

              JULIET
          You going somewhere?

              ROMEO
          I'm gonna have a
          beer with the guys.

              JULIET
          You're going out?
          I thought we could
          spend some time
          together tonight.

              ROMEO
          Hey, I worked my ass
          off today. I deserve
          a little time off
          from the grind. If
          you fixed up the place
          a little and took a
          shower every once in
          a while, maybe I'd
          stay here.

              JULIET
          What, you think I'm
          playing Wheel of
          Fortune here while

                    JULIET (CONT'D)
           you're talking to
           people and making
           eyes at the girls
           and sneaking drinks
           and stuff to your
           homeboys.

Romeo kisses baby Romeo on the top of his
head, then sits down. He takes up his cutlery
and starts banging them on the table.

                    JULIET
           What's the matter
           with you, I'm coming.

                    ROMEO
           I said I wanted dinner
           on the table.

                    JULIET
           I want a lot of things
           and I don't seem to
           be getting them either.

She slams a dish of the spaghetti on the table.

                    ROMEO
           Spaghetti, again!

Romeo flips the plate onto the floor. Juliet
looks at him.

                    JULIET
           Are you crazy?

                    ROMEO
          No, just hungry.
          Hungry and tired
          of your bullshit.

He storms out of the room. Baby Romy starts
to cry.

                    JULIET
          Where are you going?

                    ROMEO
          To get what I need
          for a change.

                    JULIET
          What about me?

                    ROMEO
          Aren't you already
          getting what you
          need from Vicente!

The door slams in the living room and Juliet
looks down at the pile of broken plate and
spaghetti on the floor.

                    JULIET
          Don't worry, Romy.
          This ain't gonna
          happen again.

To Do

Now take a scene from your own script and pare it down to its bare minimum. Be just as brutal.

Not much left to go. The hard part is over for this draft. How about giving yourself a pat on the back? Arm not long enough? How about taking yourself and someone you like out to dinner? Better yet, how about letting that person take *you* out? Then apply your butt to the chair again and finish up.

CHAPTER 8

WHERE AM I?

I congratulate you. First of all, you have read this far. Second, you may have already completed your rewrite. But now it's time to take your script's temperature and see if you can take it off intensive care. It's time to do a Script Status Report (SSR).

The purpose of the SSR is to truly know where you are, at least in your own estimation, before you start making "I'm finished!" noises. Here's an opportunity to develop some distance from your script. Objectivity is hard to achieve, but, for the moment, pretend that someone else wrote your script, then read it again. Yep. Again. And, as usual, I'll wait until you're done.

Back already? Fast reader. Okay, now it's time to see how objective you really are. Please fill out the following as honestly as possible.

SCRIPT STATUS REPORT

Project name:

What is the premise of your script in one sentence (theme or idea, not story)?

Who is the main character in one sentence?

What does he think he wants? What does he really want?

Who is preventing him from achieving that?

What inside of him is preventing him from achieving that?

What does he have to learn about himself? Others?

Who are the other main players? What are their needs?

What is the genre of your script?

What is the everyday life of the protagonist?

What is the inciting incident?

What is the Act One curtain?

What is the midpoint?

What is the Act Two curtain (the low point)?

What is the final challenge?

What is the return to (the now-changed-forever) normal life?

What is working?

What is not working?

What must change?

Happy with what you read? Good. Go to the next chapter.

Not so happy? Okay. Not unusual. Remember how many drafts I told you some writers go through? You may have a few drafts to go. For now, go back and really work on "What is not working?" When you're satisfied that the script represents the best that you can do, go to the next chapter.

Chapter 9

THE
RIGHT
LOOK

You've read my comments earlier about there being no rules in screenplay writing, just guidelines. If you follow the guidelines, you'll have a professional reading and looking script. But that doesn't necessarily guarantee a great, or even good, script. There are many times when it's a good idea to go outside of convention, to surprise your reader in both form and content.

Shane Black, for example, went outside of the rules in *Lethal Weapon* when he talked directly to the reader, addressing them as "boys and girls" and "folks." He even describes a posh Beverly Hills house as "The kind of house I'll buy if this movie is a big hit." Thousands of neophyte screenwriters have copied that technique in spec scripts ever since, to the point where it's no longer fresh, much less unique, and is considered by many to be just plain derivative. He became a parody of his own style with *Kiss Kiss, Bang Bang* when he talked to the audience in narration. But when he first did it, it suddenly engaged a reader like never before.

If you do it, you'll get slammed. You're not Shane Black. But you can still color outside the lines for effect, so long as you don't overdo it. You need to know where the lines are first. To understand what's expected, I suggest you have a look at *The Complete Screenwriters Manual* by Stephen Bowles, Ronald Mangravite, and Peter Zorn, *A Practical Guide to Flawless Screenplay*

Form by Janna Gelfand, or *The Hollywood Standard: The Complete & Authoritative Guide to Script Format and Style* by Christopher Riley. Know the conventions, but don't be afraid to blow them off for effect or to improve the flow of your story.

For example, separate slug lines within a scene can really slow down the reader. It's true that you should write a new scene line or slug line for every change of time or place, but sometimes that just distracts from the story. And while a script is a technical document (like architectural blueprints), it's also a vehicle for the imagination, like an architectural rendering. So, for example, say we're back in the apartment with Romeo and Juliet. We can establish that time and place with the initial slug line for the scene:

```
INT. R&J'S APARTMENT - DAY
```

But if we move from the living room to the hallway to the bedroom, we can assume the reader is going to know where we are and just use a few words to tell us where we're going:

```
Romeo stomps down the
HALLWAY
And tramps into the
BEDROOM
Where he sees Baby Romeo playing on the floor
with a broken lamp.
```

Technically, he's moved from one set to another, so normally we'd have a separate slug line for each room, but let's allow the director to make the decision about how it's shot (and he could have it all pre-lit and shoot it in one smooth take or he could have a series of shots — his call). Right now, what we're interested in is the speed with which the story moves.

Another way to make your story flow faster is to remove CUT TOs and DISSOLVE TOs. Why? Because every change of scene is at least a cut. If it's anything more than that, let the editor and the director work on it. If you're trying to show passage of time, you could use DISSOLVE TOs, but you'd be better off just showing how time passed by having something in the visual tell that — cigarettes butts where there were none, half-finished food on plates, various states of dress or undress (whatever is called for in the scene).

To Do
Go through your script and see if there aren't places you can speed up by cutting down on slug lines and removing CUT TOs and DISSOLVE TOs.

Spling, Gramma, Punkchewayshun, and Cents
It's easy to make mistakes in spelling, grammar, punctuation, and cents. See, I just did it again, and spellcheck wouldn't have caught it. However, mistakes tend to bounce a reader out of the story. And you don't want anything to interrupt the flow. If you have several errors on a page, the reader will (rightly) feel that

you are unprofessional and that you didn't think it worthy of your time to take care of the details of writing the script. And if you didn't think it worthy of your time, why would it be worthy of her time to read it? It could also simply mean you haven't mastered your craft. If that's the case, why should they read any further, since if you haven't mastered the basics, they have no reason to believe you've mastered the hard stuff like characterization and story telling.

"Yeah, but that's the small stuff, and I don't sweat the small stuff."

Sure, that's an attitude you could reasonably have. After all, the story is what's important, right? The big picture. The heart. The emotion.

And you'd be right to think that. Just as you'd be right to think, when you buy an automobile, it's the engine and the line of the car that are important. But would you buy a new car that's covered in scratches? Why not? It runs, doesn't it? But wouldn't you be suspicious of how it runs? Would you even take the time to take it on a test drive? What if the door handle fell off in your hand? What if the speedometer was put in upside down? Sure, the salesman could tell you all that could be fixed, but would you really want the ride?

Of course not, because it would be obvious to you that the car company hadn't finished the car. So why even bother with a test drive?

Same thing applies to a script. Do your homework. Make it look good. Proofread it. Have a friend (or better yet, a professional) proofread it. Then proofread it again. Make sure you've spelled everything correctly. Make sure that where you need to be, you are grammatically correct and that the punctuation is correct. But how do you know what is correct?

Use a dictionary. A good one. Check any word that you have any doubt about whatsoever. Use a good grammar book. The one that comes to mind is Strunk and White's *The Elements of Style*. It will help you on both grammar and punctuation.

One more note on punctuation. Why is it so important? Because it helps you clarify your intentions and emphasis. It guides the actor as well as the reader to an interpretation of your text. It sets the rhythm of the character's speech. Look at the following and see if they have different meanings depending on punctuation.

```
                     PHILLIP
Why do you want to go there you have it so
good here?


                     PHILLIP
Why? Do you want to go there? You have it so
good here.


                     PHILLIP
Why do you want to go? There you have it so
good. Here.


                     PHILLIP
Why do you want to go there? You have it so
good here.


                     PHILLIP
Why do you want to go? There you have it. So,
good. Here!
```

And you probably could think of a few more ways to punctuate this very simple sentence. But why leave its interpretation up to the reader? It's your story. Tell the reader what you mean. Don't make her guess.

To Do
Go through your script very carefully and check for spelling, punctuation, and grammar. Remember, you can break

grammatical rules if it serves you, and if you do it on purpose. If it's not intentional, you'll just look unprofessional.

Note: The rules don't apply in the same way to dialogue. Your characters should speak with the grammar appropriate to their education, class, and context.

Focusing the Reader's Attention

For some reason, movies today are considered to be a director's medium. If that were truly so, you would be able to hand a director 120 blank pieces of paper, and he would be able to fashion a film from that. Not that I have anything against directors (sometimes I am one myself), but it all stems from the word. Still, they are very protective of their domain, and development executives are enablers in this overprotection, so they don't like to see directing in a script.

How would you direct in a script? By writing camera angles: CLOSE UP, MEDIUM SHOT, TRAVELING SHOT. By writing too much business for an actor (unless it was important for the scene): Charlie swallows his donut, takes another bite and chews. He looks at the donut, shakes his head, and takes another bite. Then he chews some more.

All you really need to say is Charlie eats a doughnut while he listens to Betty. The director and the actor will fill in the rest.

But there are times when it's necessary to know how carefully Charlie chews his donut, in which case you may specify. There are even more cases when it's important to you what the reader focuses on in the scene. That's when you'd just love to use CLOSE UP, or MEDIUM SHOT, or even POV (which some people still use). How to do that without doing that? How to focus a reader without seeming to step on the director or cinematographer's feet? How about this scene:

INT. CAFETERIA - DAY

The place is jammed with college students, mostly FEMALE, mostly provocatively dressed.

JESSIE,

A 19-year-old vixen, wears a short top and pants riding as low as her anatomy will allow. She reaches for her

PHONE

Puts it to her ear.

                    JESSIE
          Name dial. Tiffany. Yes.

PHONE RING

But it sounds like an elevator gong. And it's directly across the table.

TIFFANY

A slovenly girl dressed in black, pulls her phone from her book bag.

                    TIFFANY
     What?

Do you see how we moved the reader's imagination from a wide shot of the cafeteria to a close up of Jessie to an extreme close up of her phone, to a close shot of Tiffany? We did this by calling out in caps and setting on its own line the important thing we wanted the reader to focus on.

To Do

Go through your script (again!) and cull out the camera directions. Decide what you want the reader to see in each scene and call out the individual shots. Don't overdo it, as that will lengthen your screenplay and become tiresome. Just do it enough to give it a visual pop.

Pacing

A lot has been said by screenwriting teachers and authors of screenwriting books about pacing. Some writers relentlessly turn up the juice page after page, creating a pace that is wearing on the reader. Others have no concept or control of pacing so that their scripts are great antidotes to sleepless nights. My view on pacing is that there must be ups and downs from scene to scene, sequence to sequence, with, of course, rising action, moments of frenetic action, and moments of rest.

First of all, what is rising action?

The concept is clear enough – things must get more and more difficult for your protagonist. The action (of whatever kind — martial combat or marital combat) must get progressively more intense as your movie develops. If you have the toughest battle in the first act, where do you go from there? If you maintain the same level of intensity throughout, without turning up the gas, how do you expect a reader/viewer to maintain interest? So you must save your biggest, baddest battle for the final challenge, and you must work your way up to that.

But there are important events, battles if you will, along the way. And, sometimes, you must give your reader a little respite after the most intense scenes. So you should slow down the action a little, let the reader catch her breath, throw in some comic relief (there's a reason for the 2,500-year-old tradition of comic relief), and just rest.

Then pick up the pace just as the reader is lulled into a false sense of security.

To Do
Check the pacing of your story. If you could graph it, it would look like a series of mountain peaks with sharp fall offs and gradual rises to the next peak. Is that how it feels to you when you read it?

CHAPTER 10

FINISHING

When is a script ready? Michael Colleary, co-writer with Mike Werb of *Face/Off*, answers this question by saying, "When you acknowledge it's never going to be done. When it's been proofread. When it looks like it's been written by a professional writer."

Robin Schiff says it's "When I've run out of something to do."

Ron Bass says, "When I decide it's the right time to go out, it is the right time to go out."

In other words, you know when you know, according to them. But what about you? They have years of experience and lots of people to show their scripts to for feedback before they release it to their agents or studios, even when they're on assignment. So what should you do if you haven't yet developed a cadre of trusted advisors?

Develop one.

As soon as possible. I've mentioned this before — that they should know something about writing, that they should be able to help you solve problems, and that they *not* be parents, friends, or significant others. If you join a writers group on the ground or online, you should be able to meet a few writers of similar or more experience that would be willing to trade a read for a read. That means you have to be willing to do the same, but that's a good thing. You can always learn from reading, whether it's a good script or a bad one.

Let's say you're ready now to send your child out into the Arctic winter. I mean, you're ready to send your script out to an agent or a producer. I'm asking you to give it one more read before you do. Actually, I'm asking you to give it eight quick reads. These don't have to be complete reads, as you'll see by the list, because you will be reading for different things each time. In fact, you might even call these reads "passes," as you'll be passing through the script quickly looking at very specific issues.

To Do

1. Read for structure. Make sure your seven points (see Chapter One) are fully realized and balanced in terms of page length. Make sure your scenes have a beginning, middle, and end.

2. Make sure the scenes have conflict and that they move the story forward. Cut any scenes that don't.

3. Read your descriptive paragraphs again. Are they terse? Do they move the story? Do they tell the story in images? Are they grammatically correct when they need to be?

4. There are three separate reads for dialogue. In each, you should ask yourself if you can show it rather than say it. In other words, could your characters be doing something instead of talking about it? Then you'll ask if each word — I mean each "a" and "the" — is necessary. The first dialogue pass is for the main character. Read each of his speeches and only his speeches. Are they consistent in voice? Could another character have said those words? Does his voice stand out from the crowd?

5. Do the same for the antagonist.

6. Do the same for supporting characters.

7. Go over the whole script one more time and look for cuts. Delete any non-essential scenes, cut heads and tails off of scenes if possible, cut down dialogue whenever possible.

8. And do the final spelling, punctuation, grammar, and
sense pass.

ONE MORE THING

I know you're about to kill me. "How many times do I have to
revise this thing?" you're probably saying to yourself. A professional writer might revise a script 30 times, and still, when she
hands it to a producer, the producer finds something more to
change. In fact, a script isn't done until the final cut is made, and
it goes into wide release. Even then, some writers would like to
do more. But I'm saying there's just two more areas to look at,
and that's it.

It's often said that the first five pages are the most important pages in the script. This is true because they are the pages
that engage the reader. Translated to film, they are the first five
minutes of the film. And don't you usually make up your mind
if you're going to enjoy a film by the first five minutes? Don't
you get sucked in or left out by that time?

So you have to polish and polish your first five minutes
until they're diamond-like. They have to be engaging in style
and story, and they have to introduce your character so that she's
likeable or fascinating. You have to make your reader want to
spend two hours in the dark with these people.

The last five pages are the most important five pages in
the script. Wait a second, didn't I just say the first five pages were
the most important? Yes, I did. But I've learned to live with this
contradiction in my mind because I know it to be true. The
last five pages are the most important because they must create
a lasting memory for the audience (or reader) as they leave the
theater or finish the read. They are what the audience is going
to talk about over coffee or martinis later that night, or at the
water cooler the next day. You want them to have something to
think about or something to say about the final challenge. You
want to work your film so that the closing visual makes such

an impact that the viewer can't wait to tell others about your story.

To Do

Read the first five and the last five pages over. Are these pages the absolute best you can do? If you're not sure, make them better. If you're sure, now's the time to send out your script.

But first, register it with the WGA, West, online at *www.wgawregistry.org*. Now you can send it out.

Okay, *one more thing*. Read over the script status report you completed in Chapter Eight. Have you dealt with all the issues you described then? If not, refer to the table of contents for help on those areas. Rewrite what you need to rewrite. Then you're done.

To Whom?

Now comes the hard part — selling the pile of paper you've put all those ink marks on. So, who do you give it to now?

To answer that, you might start with Kathie Fong Yoneda's book, *The Script Selling Game: A Hollywood Insider's Look at Getting Your Script Sold and Produced* (Michael Wiese Productions). You might start with a list of franchised agents available from the Writers Guild of America, West, on their website, *www.wga.org*. You might just ask around, using your network of writers. You might ask your Uncle Harry (who knows, maybe he knows the assistant to the valet at the restaurant where Brad Pitt's agent's assistant likes to get late-night snacks.). But whatever you do, don't let it sit in your desk drawer. You've written a script because you had a story to tell. You can't tell your story unless someone reads it. So get someone to read it. Anyone. And ask everyone you know if they know someone else who will read it, preferably someone with some connection to the film business.

Then, if all goes well, and the stars are in alignment, a producer will buy it. And ask for a rewrite.

At least you'll know where to start.

And you'll be ready.

But before you start on the next draft, celebrate this one. It was probably more work than you anticipated, but it's much better, isn't it? So reward yourself big time. It was a big job and you deserve something commensurate. A weekend away with nothing to do (it may be hard to do, but force yourself). Just relax, recharge, reinvigorate. Enjoy. That's part of the process, too.

APPENDIX A
THE SEVEN POINTS OF *THELMA & LOUISE*

1. **Ordinary Life**
   Thelma starts off as the repressed housewife to car sales-
   man/district manager Darryl, a male chauvinist pig if
   there ever was one. She even has to ask his permission
   to go away for the weekend with her friend, Louise, a
   waitress with an attitude and a steady boyfriend.

2. **Inciting Incident**
   When a stranger takes Thelma outside a country bar to
   get some air, he tries to rape her, but Louise stops it by
   putting a bullet through the man's heart.

3. **End of Act One**
   Thelma agrees to go to Mexico after she tells Darryl to
   "go fuck yourself."

4. **Midpoint or Turning Point**
   Thelma has a sexual awakening with J. D., but he also
   steals their cash. Thelma takes charge, and they go on a
   crime spree.

5. **The Low Point**
   Thelma learns that the police know they're going to
   Mexico. They're doomed.

6. **The Final Challenge**
   Thelma suggests that they don't give up and get caught,
   that they should keep goin'. They kiss, hold hands, and
   drive into the canyon.

7. **The Return to (the Now–Changed–Forever) Normal
   Life**
   Thelma and Louise are dead, but they are free of men
   for the first time. The implication is that the audience is
   now changed forever because of their journey.

APPENDIX B
BEATSHEET — IN GOOD COMPANY, SCREENPLAY BY PAUL WEITZ

Ordinary Life:

1. Dan Forman goes through the ordinary morning routine and finds out from the news that his magazine has been bought by Teddy K.

2. He also discovers an empty pregnancy test box and thinks his daughter might be pregnant.

3. Dan visits one of his biggest clients, but the client decides to pull his advertising from Dan's magazine.

4. Carter Duryea presents a new marketing strategy for dinosaur phones just as his boss announces he's leaving to head up marketing at the magazine Teddy K has bought. Carter asks to be taken along, and he is.

5. Dan returns home and tries to get his daughter to open up to him (about possible pregnancy).

6. Dan goes to bed, but his wife is up. He asks about his daughter Alex. But his wife tells him she's pregnant. Though he can't believe it at first, he's happy.

7. Carter is excited, but his wife wants him to shut up and go to sleep. She questions his qualifications for the job.

8. Others in Dan's office worry they're going to get fired. Dan gets demoted, his job taken by Carter.

9. Carter and Alex meet in the magazine's elevator. He confesses that he doesn't know what he's doing. She likes that.

Inciting Incident Sequence:

10. In the office, Dan bumps into Carter by accident. Instead of staying, Dan goes to play tennis with Alex.

11. In an age versus youth match, Alex kicks his butt. Then she tells him she's transferring to NYU and will live in the city. Though it's going to be difficult, he agrees to the increased expense.

12. Carter is shown around the office, then shown his office — it's Dan's.

13. Dan returns to find him there. He's 26 and he's Dan's new boss. Dan responds by throwing a baseball at a trophy after Carter leaves.

14. The name plates are changed on the office door, and the offices are moved.

15. Carter buys a new Porsche. He immediately gets into an accident.

16. When he gets home, his wife leaves him.

17. At the obstetrician's office, Dan has an attack of arrhythmia and tells his wife, Ann, for the first time that he's been demoted.

18. Carter spends the night in his new car after a fast-food meal.

End of Act One

19. After downing a couple of lattes, Carter has trouble leading a sales meeting. But he comes up with an idea to synergize the sales force and increase sales by 20%. His goal.

Act Two

20. Carter takes Dan to a sushi restaurant and forces some sushi on him. He offers him the job of being his "wing man," though Dan doesn't see the merit of that. However, if he takes the position, he'll keep his job.

21. The first man Carter fires is the office kiss-up, who leaves angrily.

22. Carter shows himself to be a lonely workaholic in a series of shots. In one, he puts Dan down at a meeting.

23. Before a meeting, Carter's boss comes and tells Carter he's got to fire some more people. Carter's not happy about it.

24. As the meeting breaks up, Carter desperately tries to get someone to go for a drink with him, but no takers. Inadvertently, Dan invites him to dinner.

25. Carter is ecstatic to be there, but he makes a bad impression on Ann. Dan just wants to get rid of him. Dan and Ann discuss how they're going to meet the new college expenses.

26. Carter meets Alex in the living room. She's somewhat hostile. He admits that it's the anniversary of the first date with his wife. His honesty impresses her.

27. In the kitchen, Ann and Dan argue about Alex at NYU, then Dan drops the ziti on the floor and Ann pukes.

28. Alex and Carter play foosball and talk about peaking too early.

29. The pizza arrives and Dan gets his younger daughter off the phone. Dan calls Alex and Carter, the "kids," in for dinner.

30. At the table, there's some embarrassing conversation, and then Carter spills his drink into Dan's lap. Carter and Alex share a moment.

31. Carter reluctantly leaves, and Alex watches from the window.

32. Alone at his house, Carter feels alone.

33. Dan helps Alex move to the dorm at NYU.

34. Carter moves to a new apartment in the city.

35. Dan says goodbye to Alex after giving her pepper spray. He struggles to hold back the tears.

36. In matching scenes, Ann and Dan sign mortgage papers while Carter signs divorce papers.

37. Carter forces Dan to take some clients to the corporate box to a concert instead of a game and tells him he has to sell more pages or some people will be let go. They disagree on the use of the term "let go."

38. At the concert, the client is uncomfortable with the atmosphere, but good with Dan. When they sneak out, the client informs him that his mega-corp is feuding with Dan's mega-corp, and he can't do business with him anymore.

39. Carter tells Dan he has to fire Louie and Morty... or him.

40. Dan goes home to his family, Carter sleeps on the couch at work.

41. Dan fires Morty and Louie. They don't take it well.

42. Dan turns in his own evaluation. He doesn't meet expectations.

43. Morty and Louie leave the office. Everyone's sad.

Midpoint

44. Carter bumps into Alex at an outdoor café. He has coffee with her. They hit it off and go for a walk.

45. They spend the day and she invites him to her dorm room after kissing him.

46. Alex seduces a reluctant Carter, and he succumbs.

47. In the office the next morning, Dan calls him jumpy, but Carter denies.

48. In a montage, Alex and Carter play tennis, go out for coffee, etc. Carter fires more people. Dan tries calling Alex between shopping trips.

49. In an intramural basketball match, Dan meets Carter's boss, Mark, who's a jerk. There's a ringer on Mark's team. It's a rough game, and Dan gets injured in a dunk attempt.

50. Dan has concerns about getting in touch with his daughter which Carter allays. Carter asks Dan for advice on keeping a marriage going.

51. Dan's family surprises him with a birthday party. He takes a minute to enter, then comes in wearing only his boxers. Surprise!

52. Dan talks to Morey, who isn't doing well, though his wife got a raise.

53. Carter meets with Alex in his car. He gives her an expensive necklace and tells her she's the kind of girl that it's good to be in a foxhole with (harkening to advice Dan had given him).

54. Later, opening his gifts, Dan discovers that Carter and Alex are together.

Low Point

55. Dan follows Carter to a restaurant and finds him there with Alex. He slugs him in a confrontation and has words with his daughter.

56. Carter goes to Alex's dorm, but she breaks up with him.

Act Three

57. When Dan returns home, he finds that Ann is in the hospital. He goes there, and it was just a scare about the baby.

58. At the hospital, Alex and Dan make up. She tells him he doesn't have to change, but he maintains that he does.

59. At the office, Teddy K shares his vision of the future with everyone. Dan challenges his thinking to his face. Teddy K leaves it to Dan and the others to answer Dan's questions.

60. Mark storms into Dan's office and fires him. Carter resigns, too, but tells him he'll call Teddy K to tell him how Mark's driven the magazine into the ground. They get a short reprieve.

Final Challenge

61. Dan and Carter visit Mr. Kalb and convince him to make a major ad buy in the magazine.

62. When they return, they find that Teddy K has sold the company to a rival. Mark and Carter lose their jobs, but Dan gets his old one back.

63. As Dan moves back into his office, Carter walks the streets, thinking.

Return to Normal, Now-Changed-Forever, Life

64. Carter returns to the office a month later in sweats and goes to see Dan. Carter turns down Dan's office to come back to work as his second in command, but acknowledges that Dan has done a lot for him. They part with a heartfelt hug.

65. At the elevator, he bumps into Alex, who's coming to play tennis with Dan. They have a tense conversation in front of Morty, who reminds them that timing is everything.

66. At the hospital, Dan announces to his daughters that they have a baby sister. He's "psyched."

67. Carter gets a call from Dan while actually jogging outside at the beach. They talk like old friends.

APPENDIX C

The first five pages, written and rewritten, of *Youngsters*, written by Paul Chitlik for Rysher Entertainment for the Olsen Twins, under the supervision of James Orr and Jim Cruickshank, writers of *Tough Guys*, *Man of the House*, *Mr. Destiny*, *Sister Act 2*, and *Three Men and a Baby*.

The first set of pages is from a draft near the end of my eight passes on the first draft that I thought was too fat. Notes on the pages are my own.

YOUNGSTERS

Written by

Paul Chitlik

ACT I

DRAFT
4/10/96

April 12, 1996

FADE IN:

ON A COPY MACHINE TRAY

as page after page of legal papers come snapping into
place. Suddenly, the copier comes to a halt.

                    ALICE (OS)
          Damn!

INT. LAW OFFICES (COPY ROOM) - DAY

Small, cramped. Reams of paper and supplies stacked.
Two large copiers, one on either side of the room. And

ALICE BURDOCK,

early 40's, skirt and blouse (we'll see the suit jacket
in her office), turns from one of the copiers where she
was loading something page by page. She looks at the
copier that stopped. There's a hand printed sign on it

          "Controller bad. Hold 'Start' button
               down for multiple copies."

                    ALICE
          Okay, I'll hold the start button.

She presses the start button and the machine starts up
again. While she's holding it, she reaches over to
continue copying some other document page by page, but
she can't reach the machine to lift the cover and hold
the button at the same time. Every time she takes her
finger off the start button, the machine stops. A
dilemma.

She lifts her leg to try to use her foot to press the
button, but her skirt's a little too tight for that. So
she hikes her skirt up, puts one foot on the button,
leans over and starts working the other machine, page
by page... Both machines are going now.

                    KATHY (OS)
          Exactly what part of your body are
          you trying to Xerox?

Alice looks up to see KATHY, 40's, more secretarial.
She's got some papers in her hands. Alice immediately
takes her leg down.

                    ALICE

                    (embarrassed)
          Oh, hi, Kathy. There's a short in
          the start switch so you have to
          hold it and...

                    KATHY
          Or you could do what I do.

     She walks over to a work surface, takes some scotch
     tape off a roll and fastens it on the switch under...

                    KATHY (Cont'd)
          I just love lawyers. They're so
          practical. Where's Marta?

                    ALICE
          Typing a motion that has to be in
          by close of business.

     The machine starts rolling again as Alice works the
     other one page by page.

                    KATHY
          Not going to the party for Roz?

                    ALICE
          Got things to do.

                    KATHY
          What for? You're never going to
          make partner here.

                    ALICE
          Thanks. Coming from you, that
          means a lot to me.

                    KATHY
          Haven't you figured out he's
          passed you up for a reason?

                    ALICE
          And that would be?

                    KATHY
          You won't put up a fuss. He wants
          Goldilocks for her image. She's
          young.

                    ALICE
          I'm young.

                    KATHY
          Younger.

                        ALICE
          Are we talking policy or
          consistent age discrimination
          here?

                        KATHY
          I don't know what you're talking
          about. I'm an employee. I follow
          orders.

                        ALICE
          That's comforting.
Kathy just shrugs her shoulders like, "Whaddya gonna
do?"

                        KATHY
          Reality is mean when it strikes
          you in the face.

The copier stops again.

                        ALICE
          You've been a big help, Kathy.

Alice presses the copy button again, and this time the
copies come shooting out the copy tray all over the
floor faster than she can react.

INT. CORRIDOR - A MOMENT LATER

as Alice walks down the hallway with a stack of papers
in her hands.

In the glass walled conference/board room, several
ATTORNEYS, MALE and FEMALE, have gathered. The door's
open to the room, and WE HEAR the tinkle of glasses and
the excited and congratulatory conversation leak into
the corridor as Alice walks by.

Several OLDER PARTNERS are toasting ROSALYN ECKERT,
late 20's/early 30's. Some of the chatter we hear is
about being the youngest partner ever...

Alice looks back, then continues on down the hall.
Her tone changes from being in a hurry to being angry
and in a hurry.

INT. LAW OFFICES - CONTINUOUS

as Alice charges down a row of secretarial cubicles.
She stops at the entrance to one and drops half her
papers on the desk.

ALICE
Copier jammed. Could you take it
from page 37? I haven't got time
to do it now.

MARTA continues typing as if nobody were there.

ALICE (Cont'd)
Thanks. I'll read the first half
tonight and get the rest in the
morning.

Alice continues into her office...

INT. ~~LAW OFFICES~~ ALICE'S OFFICE - CONTINUOUS

as she grabs files and papers and stuffs them into her
briefcase. In the background, we can still hear the
celebration. On her cluttered desk, a picture of her
and her daughter, JENNA, 10, and a copy of "Stop Aging
Now!" next to a copy of "Organize Your Desk, Organize
Your Life."

Alice opens the top drawer of her desk to get a pencil.
WE SEE a jumble of things, including a bottle of Oil of
Olay, a tube of Retin A, and other products for
"younger skin."

R.J. (OS)
Leaving early?

R.J., an Armani suited man in his fifties, sticks his
head into the doorway.

R.J.
I was hoping we could talk about
the Kidco In-line Skates liability
case.

ALICE
Sorry, R.J. ~~Maybe~~ Tomorrow. I
can't tonight. My ex had to go
out of town on business at the
last minute, so I have to pick up
Jenna.

R.J.
Jenna?

ALICE
My daughter.

                    R.J.
Oh.
    (then)
We missed you at Roz's thing.

                    ALICE
I missed *me* at Roz's thing.

                    R.J.
What's that?

                    ALICE
I mean, I just had to finish up a
few things before I left.

                    R.J.
Look, Alice. I know you're upset
about not making partner before
Roz. I'm sorry.

                    ALICE
Thanks, R.J. I'll take that to
the market and see how many bags
of groceries can I get for a "My
boss is sorry."

                    R.J.
I don't like that tone, young
lady.

                    ALICE
Look, R.J. I've busted my butt
for this firm. I deserve the
money and the corner office. I
deserve partner. And you know it.

                    R.J.
Prove it. If you win the Kidco
case, it'll happen for you. But
you won't win unless you give it
your full attention.

                    ALICE
My full attention?

He looks at his watch, then over to her packing her
briefcase.

                    R.J.
I think you know what I mean.

He exits. Alice pauses for a moment, then jams a
couple of file folders into her briefcase.

Here's the version after the notes have been entered. Sometimes, there are even subtle changes in this process.

YOUNGSTERS

Written by

Paul Chitlik

April 15, 1996

FADE IN:

ON A COPY MACHINE TRAY

as page after page of legal papers come snapping into
place. Suddenly, the copier comes to a halt.

                        ALICE (OS)
            Damn!

INT. LAW OFFICES (COPY ROOM) - DAY

Small, cramped. Reams of paper and supplies stacked.
Two large copiers, one on either side of the room. And

ALICE BURDOCK,

early 40's, skirt and blouse (we'll see the suit jacket
in her office), turns from one of the copiers where she
was loading something page by page. She looks at the
copier that stopped. There's a hand printed sign on it

            "Controller bad. Hold 'Start' button
                down for multiple copies."

                        ALICE
            Okay, I'll hold the start button.

She presses the start button and the machine starts up
again. While she's holding it, she reaches over to
continue copying some other document page by page, but
she can't reach the machine to lift the cover and hold
the button at the same time. Every time she takes her
finger off the start button, the machine stops. A
dilemma.

She lifts her leg to try to use her foot to press the
button, but her skirt's a little too tight for that, so
she hikes her skirt up, puts one foot on the button,
leans over and, in an incredible balancing act, starts
working the other machine, page by page... Both
machines are going now.

                        KATHY (OS)
            Exactly what part of your body are
            you trying to Xerox?

Alice looks up to see KATHY, 40's, secretarial. She's
got some papers in her hands. Alice immediately takes
her leg down.

ALICE
(embarrassed)
Oh, hi, Kathy. There's a short in
the start switch so you have to
hold it and...

KATHY
Or you could do what I do.

She walks over to a work surface, takes some scotch
tape off a roll and fastens it on the switch under...

KATHY (Cont'd)
I just love lawyers. They're so
practical.

The machine starts rolling again as Alice works the
other one page by page.

KATHY
Not going to the party for Roz?

ALICE
Got things to do.

KATHY
Why bust your butt for these guys?
You're never going to make partner.

ALICE
Oh?

KATHY
Haven't you figured out he's
passed you up for a reason?

ALICE
And that would be?

KATHY
He wants Miss Goldilocks for her
image. She's young. And he knows
you won't put up a fuss when
you're passed over.

ALICE
I'm young.

KATHY
Younger.

ALICE
Are we talking consistent age
discrimination here?

> KATHY
> I don't know what you're talking
> about. I'm an employee. I follow
> orders.

> ALICE
> That's comforting.

Kathy just shrugs her shoulders like, "Whaddya gonna
do?"

> KATHY
> Reality is mean when it strikes
> you in the face.

The copier stops again.

> ALICE
> You've been a big help, Kathy.

Alice presses the copy button again, and this time the
copies come shooting out the copy tray all over the
floor faster than she can react.

INT. CORRIDOR - A MOMENT LATER

as Alice walks down the hallway with a stack of papers
in her hands.

In the glass walled conference/board room, several
ATTORNEYS, MALE and FEMALE, have gathered. The door's
open to the room, and WE HEAR the tinkle of glasses and
the excited and congratulatory conversation leak into
the corridor as Alice walks by.

Several OLDER PARTNERS are toasting ROSALYN ECKERT,
late 20's/early 30's. Some of the chatter we hear is
about being the youngest partner ever...

Alice looks back, then continues on down the hall.
Her tone changes from being in a hurry to being angry
and in a hurry.

INT. LAW OFFICES - CONTINUOUS

as Alice charges down a row of secretarial cubicles.
She stops at the entrance to one and drops half her
papers on the desk.

                              ALICE
                Copier jammed. Could you take it
                from page 37? I haven't got time
                to do it now.

MARTA continues typing as if nobody were there.

                         ALICE (Cont'd)
                Thanks. I'll read the first half
                tonight and get the rest in the
                morning.

Marta still ignores her.

                              ALICE
                Thank you. That'll be all, Marta.

Alice continues into her office...

INT. ALICE'S OFFICE - CONTINUOUS

as she grabs files and papers and stuffs them into her
briefcase. In the background, we can still hear the
celebration. On her cluttered desk, a picture of her
and her daughter, JENNA, 10, and a copy of "Stop Aging
Now!" next to a copy of "Organize Your Desk, Organize
Your Life."

Alice opens the top drawer of her desk to get a pencil.
WE SEE a jumble of things, including a bottle of Oil of
Olay, a tube of Retin A, and other products for
"younger skin."

                           R.J. (OS)
                Leaving early?

R.J., an Armani suited man in his fifties, sticks his
head into the doorway.

                              R.J.
                I was hoping we could talk about
                the Kidco In-line Skates liability
                case.

                              ALICE
                Sorry, R.J. Tomorrow. I can't
                tonight. My ex had to go out of
                town on business at the last
                minute, so I have to pick up Jenna.

                              R.J.
                Jenna?

                         ALICE
          My daughter. You know, the one
          I've had since you hired me five
          years ago.

                         R.J.
          Oh.
                (then)
          We missed you at Roz's thing.

                         ALICE
          I missed *me* at Roz's thing.

                         R.J.
          Look, Alice. I know you're upset
          about not making partner before
          Roz. I'm sorry.

                         ALICE
          Thanks, R.J. I'll take your "I'm
          sorry" to the market and see how
          many bags of groceries can I get
          for it.

                         R.J.
          I don't like that tone, young
          lady.

                         ALICE
          Look, R.J. I've busted my butt
          for this firm. I deserve the
          money and the corner office. I
          deserve partner. And you know it.

                         R.J.
          Prove it. If you win the Kidco
          case, it'll happen for you. But
          you won't win unless you give it
          your full attention.

                         ALICE
          My full attention?

He looks at his watch, then over to her packing her
briefcase.

                         R.J.
          I think you know what I mean.

He exits. Alice pauses for a moment, then jams a
couple of file folders into her briefcase.

I decided to make a few cuts, sharpen it up a little before showing it to Orr and Cruickshank. Smaller changes, but ones that
made the whole script a faster read. See if you can spot them.

If you think reading pages that are almost, but not quite,
identical is tiresome, you might start thinking of another career.
Everything in making film and television is about minute differences: in performance, in lighting, in dialogue, in editing,
even in projection and seating. The best filmmakers take care of
the details, even if it means 20 takes, 20 cuts, or 20 drafts. Here's
another.

YOUNGSTERS

Written by

Paul Chitlik

FIRST DRAFT
April 25, 1996

FADE IN:

ON A COPY MACHINE TRAY

as page after page of legal papers come snapping into
place. Suddenly, the copier comes to a halt.

                    ALICE (OS)
          Damn!

INT. LAW OFFICES (COPY ROOM) - DAY

Small, cramped. Reams of paper and supplies stacked.
Two large copiers, one on either side of the room. And

ALICE BURDOCK,

early 40's, skirt and blouse (we'll see the suit jacket
in her office), turns from one of the copiers where she
was loading something page by page. She looks at the
copier that stopped. There's a hand printed sign on it

          "Controller bad. Hold 'Start' button
              down for multiple copies."

                    ALICE
          Okay, I'll hold the start button.

She presses the start button and the machine starts up
again. While she's holding it, she reaches over to
continue copying some other document page by page, but
she can't reach the machine to lift the cover and hold
the button at the same time. Every time she takes her
finger off the start button, the machine stops. A
dilemma.

She lifts her leg to try to use her foot to press the
button, but her skirt's a little too tight for that, so
she hikes her skirt up, puts one foot on the button,
leans over and, in an incredible balancing act, starts
working the other machine, page by page... Both
machines are going now.

                    KATHY (OS)
          Exactly what part of your body are
          you trying to Xerox?

Alice looks up to see KATHY, 30's, secretarial. She's
got some papers in her hands. Alice immediately takes
her leg down.

                    ALICE
              (embarrassed)
          Oh, hi, Kathy. There's a short in
          the start switch so you have to
          hold it and...

                    KATHY
          Or you could do what I do.

She walks over to a work surface, takes some scotch
tape off a roll and fastens it on the switch under...

                    KATHY (Cont'd)
          I just love lawyers. They're so
          practical.

The machine starts rolling again as Alice works the
other one page by page.

                    KATHY
          Not going to the party for Roz?

                    ALICE
          Got things to do.

                    KATHY
          Why bust your butt for these guys?
          You're never going to make partner.

                    ALICE
          Oh?

                    KATHY
          Haven't you figured out he's
          passed you up for a reason?

                    ALICE
          And that would be?

                    KATHY
          He likes his partners young, like
          Miss Goldilocks. Makes him look
          young.

                    ALICE
          I'm young.

                    KATHY
          Younger.

                    ALICE
          Are we talking a consistent policy
          of age discrimination here?

                              KATHY
                    I don't know what you're talking
                    about. I'm an employee. I follow
                    orders.

                              ALICE
                    That's comforting.

The copier stops again.

                              ALICE
                    You've been a big help, Kathy.

Alice presses the copy button again, and this time the
copies come shooting out the copy tray all over the
floor faster than she can react.

INT. CORRIDOR - A MOMENT LATER

as Alice walks down the hallway with a stack of papers
in her hands.

In the glass walled conference/board room, several
ATTORNEYS, MALE and FEMALE, have gathered. The door's
open to the room, and WE HEAR the tinkle of glasses and
the excited and congratulatory conversation leak into
the corridor as Alice walks by.

Several OLDER PARTNERS are toasting ROSALYN ECKERT,
late 20's/early 30's. Some of the chatter we hear is
about being the youngest partner ever...

Alice looks back, then continues on down the hall.
Her tone changes from being in a hurry to being angry
and in a hurry.

INT. LAW OFFICES - CONTINUOUS

as Alice charges down a row of secretarial cubicles.
She stops at the entrance to one and drops half her
papers on the desk.

                              ALICE
                    Copier jammed. Could you take it
                    from page 37? I haven't got time
                    to do it now.

MARTA continues typing as if nobody were there.

                              ALICE (Cont'd)
                    Thanks. I'll read the first half
                    tonight and get the rest in the morning.

Marta still ignores her.

                    ALICE
        Thank you. That'll be all, Marta.

Alice continues into her office...

INT. ALICE'S OFFICE - CONTINUOUS

as she grabs files and papers and stuffs them into her
briefcase. In the background, we can still hear the
celebration. On her cluttered desk, a picture of her
and her daughter, JENNA, 10, and a copy of "Stop Aging
Now!" next to a copy of "Organize Your Desk, Organize
Your Life."

Alice opens the top drawer of her desk to get a pencil.
WE SEE a jumble of things, including a bottle of Oil of
Olay, a tube of Retin A, and other products for
"younger skin."

                    R.J. (OS)
            Leaving early?

R.J., an Armani suited man in his fifties, sticks his
head into the doorway.

                    R.J.
            We need to talk about the Kidco
            In-line Skates liability case.

                    ALICE
            I know. I read the engineer's
            preliminary report. The high rate
            of brake failure means it *is*
            Kidco's fault children are getting
            hurt.

                    R.J.
            Screw the kids, can we get Kidco
            off the hook or not?

                    ALICE
            I'm...I'm not sure. Can we talk
            about this tomorrow?

                    R.J.
            Look, Alice. I know you're upset
            about not making partner before
            Roz. I'm sorry.

                    ALICE
          Thanks, R.J. I'll take your "I'm
          sorry" to the market and see how
          many bags of groceries can I get
          for it.

                    R.J.
          I don't like that tone, young
          lady.

                    ALICE
          Look. I've busted my butt for
          this firm. I deserve the money
          and the corner office. I deserve
          partner. And you know it.

                    R.J.
          Prove it. If you win the Kidco
          case, it'll happen for you. But
          you won't win unless you give it
          your full attention.

                    ALICE
          Sixty hours a week isn't enough?

He looks at his watch, then over to her packing her
briefcase.

                    R.J.
          Not when you leave in the middle
          of the day for personal business.
          You've got to get your priorities
          right, or you can forget about a
          future here.

He exits. Alice pauses for a moment, then angrily jams
a couple of file folders into her briefcase.

INT. LAW OFFICES (MARTA'S CUBICLE) - LATER

as Alice rushes out of the office. Marta doesn't look
up.

                    ALICE
          Patch through any calls for me,
          okay? Thanks. I don't know what
          I'd do without you.

Alice continues down the hall.

At this point, I showed Orr and Cruickshank the draft, prior to handing it in to Rysher. They suggested I focus more on Alice's main issue — her problems with growing old, both internal and external. So I did. Note the differences.

YOUNGSTERS

Written by

Paul Chitlik

FIRST DRAFT
May 6, 1996

FADE IN:

ALICE'S EYES

as she checks for wrinkles around them in the mirror.
She reaches down to the counter and WE SEE that we're
in

INT. THE RESTROOM - DAY

where ALICE BURDOCK, 30's, business suit and blouse,
pulls a tube of Preparation H from her purse, puts it
on the counter, then pulls a tube of Retin A from her
purse, squeezes out a dab, puts the tube down, and
applies it to the creases of her eyes.

As she continues working on her face, WE HEAR the flush
of a toilet and the clanking of a stall door. Alice
SEES in the mirror...

ROSALYN ECKERT, late 20's, come out of the stall.
Rosalyn is also in a suit, good looking, maybe even a
little flashy. We only see her from the front as she
approaches the sink and washes her hands under...

                    ALICE
          Roz.

                    ROSALYN
          Alice.
               (re Preparation H)
          Hemorrhoids on your face?

                    ALICE
          What? No, I'm using the Retina A.

                    ROSALYN
          I've always admired the way you
          wear your age.

                    ALICE
          My age?

Rosalyn grabs a couple of paper towels, dries her
hands.

                    ROSALYN
          You boomers are so touchy. You're
          not old... you're mature, seasoned.

                    ALICE
          You make me sound like a side of
          beef.

                    ROSALYN
          I just mean all the associates
          think of you as our... den mother.

                    ALICE
          Thanks.   That makes me feel
          better.

                    ROSALYN
          Ready for the announcement?

                    ALICE
          I have been for five years.

                    ROSALYN
          You're due, all right.

Rosalyn does a last minute check of her makeup in the
mirror.

                    ROSALYN
          I just hope you aren't
          disappointed again.

                    ALICE
          I won't be.

                    ROSALYN
          Well, you never know what's going
          to happen, do you?

                    ALICE
          No, you never know.

Rosalyn casually looks over the competition.

                    ROSALYN
          Oh, Alice.   Your shoe.   You've got
          a piece of toilet paper stuck to
          it.   Attention to detail.   An
          important trait for a partner.

                    ALICE
          Thanks for the tip.

Rosalyn turns to go as Alice removes the toilet paper
from her shoe.   Then Alice looks up and SEES that
Rosalyn has got the hem of her skirt and a toilet seat
protector accidentally tucked into the back of her panty
hose.

                    ALICE
          Oh, Roz, your--

                          ROSALYN
          Attention to detail. That's what
          separates the good from the great.

                          ALICE
          Thanks, Roz. I'll remember that.

INT. CONFERENCE ROOM

In the glass walled conference/board room, several
ATTORNEYS, MALE and FEMALE, have gathered. There's an
excited buzz going around the room as the assembled
wait for the announcement.

Alice is chatting with her SECRETARY.

Rosalyn is on the other side of the room talking with a
couple of the OLDER ATTORNEYS. Her skirt is fixed now.

R.J. breezes into the room. He's an Armani suited man
in his fifties, all smiles, in control. He clears his
throat and all conversation stops.

Alice straightens up.

                          R.J.
          I've gathered you today to honor
          an exceptional woman. A fine
          attorney, loved and respected by
          her colleagues...

Alice subtly primps, smooths her skirt, etc.

                          R.J.
          ...who possesses one of the finest
          legal minds this firm has ever had
          the good fortune to retain. I'm
          sure it's not going to come as a
          surprise to you, then to see a new
          name on our letterhead, our most
          outstanding *former* associate and
          new partner...

Alice starts to take a step forward...

                          R.J.
          Rosalyn Eckert.

Devastated, Alice leans back against the sideboard
for support.

Rosalyn beams as the others rush to congratulate her.

But Alice is crestfallen. She sidles out of the room
as the others mob Rosalyn.

INT. ALICE'S OFFICE - LATER

as she grabs files and papers and stuffs them into her
briefcase. In the background, we can still hear the
celebration. On her cluttered desk, a picture of her
and her daughter, JENNA, 10, and a copy of "Stop Aging
Now!" next to a copy of "Organize Your Desk, Organize
Your Life."

WE HEAR a knock on the open door.

                    R.J. (OS)
          Got a minute?

R. J. sticks his head into the doorway.

                    ALICE
          Only a minute, R.J. I've got to
          pick up my daughter. What is it?

                    R.J.
          Look, Alice. I know you must be
          upset about not making partner.
          I'm sorry.

                    ALICE
          Thanks, R.J. I'll take your "I'm
          sorry" to the market and see how
          many bags of groceries I can get
          for it.

                    R.J.
          It was really close, Alice. Down
          to the wire. We had a tough time
          deciding. It could have gone
          either way.

                    ALICE
          So why didn't it go my way? I've
          busted my butt for this firm. I
          deserve partner. And you know it.

                    R.J.
          It's just that Roz is better for
          the image of the company.

                    ALICE
          What you mean is, she's younger.

                    R.J.
          What I mean is, she's a hard
          worker, totally dedicated--

                    ALICE
          You're full of shit!

                    R.J.
          I know you're upset, so I forgive
          that statement.

                    ALICE
          I work sixty hours a week. Isn't
          that enough?

He looks at his watch, then over to her packing her
briefcase.

                    R.J.
               (hardening)
          Not when you leave in the middle
          of the day for personal business.
          You've got to get your priorities
          right, or you can forget about a
          future here. Is that clear?

                    ALICE
          Very.

He exits. Alice pauses for a moment, then angrily jams
a couple of file folders into her briefcase.

INT. LAW OFFICES (SECRETARY'S CUBICLE) - LATER

as Alice rushes out of the office. Her SECRETARY
doesn't look up.

                    ALICE
          Patch through any calls for me,
          okay?

No answer. Alice continues down the hall.

                    ALICE (Cont'd)
          Thanks. I don't know what I'd do
          without you.

INT. HALLWAY (ELEVATORS) - MOMENTS LATER

WE HEAR the muffled RINGING of a cellular phone.

Hurrying down the hall, Alice reaches into her purse
and pulls out a ringing cell phone...

                    ALICE
          Hello. Right. I need that
          engineer's report on my desk in
          the morning...

as Alice reaches the elevator. One hand has the
briefcase, the other holds up the cell phone. She
doesn't have a free hand to punch the elevator call
button. She leans down and punches the elevator button
with her nose.

                    ALICE
          I understand, but that doesn't
          mean... No, just a stuffy nose...
          The preliminary report says the
          brakes may not work properly if...

The elevator door opens and Alice enters talking.

EXT. JENNA'S SCHOOL - DAY

It's warm out on this early fall day. The school bell
RINGS and BOYS and GIRLS pour out of the front door.

JENNA

age ten, carrying a backpack with a laptop computer
sticking out of it, bounds out of the front door with a
friend, SUSIE, also 10. Jenna looks around, doesn't
see her mother. Susie looks around... nobody for her.

                    SUSIE
          Captain, the parental units are
          late for the rendezvous, and
          scanners aren't picking up any
          shuttles in the quadrant.

                    JENNA
          My mom's working on a big product
          liability case. She's always
          late, everywhere.

The girls take seats on the steps as other STUDENTS
exit the school and meet with PARENTS or just walk down
the street in groups.

                    SUSIE
          My mom just *likes* to be late. My
          dad says it's like a thing with
          her.

One more go around to sharpen it up before handing it over to Rysher. I wanted to make sure it was the best draft I could do to give it the best chance to get the film made. This next draft was to sharpen the dialogue and emphasize the humor.

YOUNGSTERS

Written by

Paul Chitlik

FIRST DRAFT
May 10, 1996

FADE IN:

ALICE'S EYES

as she checks for wrinkles around them in the mirror.
She reaches down to the counter and WE SEE that we're
in

INT. THE RESTROOM - DAY

where ALICE BURDOCK, 30's, business suit and blouse,
pulls a tube of Retin A from her purse, squeezes out a
dab, puts the tube down, and applies it to the creases
of her eyes.

As she continues working on her face, WE HEAR the flush
of a toilet and the clanking of a stall door. Alice
SEES in the mirror...

ROSALYN ECKERT, late 20's, come out of the stall.
Rosalyn is also in a suit, good looking, maybe even a
little flashy. We only see her from the front as she
approaches the sink and washes her hands under...

                    ALICE
          Roz.

                    ROSALYN
          Alice.

Alice continues applying the cream. It's clear from
Roz's tone that they're competitors, and everything
that Roz says is really meant as a cut and not a
compliment.

                    ROSALYN (Cont'd)
          You don't need to do that. Those
          little lines add character to your
          face.

                    ALICE
          You saying I'm wrinkled?

                    ROSALYN
          I'm just saying you wear your age
          well.

                    ALICE
          So now you're saying I'm old.

Rosalyn grabs a couple of paper towels, dries her
hands.

                    ROSALYN
You boomers are so touchy. You're
not old... you're mature, seasoned.

                    ALICE
You make me sound like a side of
beef.

                    ROSALYN
I just mean all the associates
think of you as our... den mother.

                    ALICE
Thanks. That makes me feel
a lot better.

                    ROSALYN
We all figure you're the one
R.J.'s going to announce as the
new partner today.

                    ALICE
I hope that's what R.J. figures.

                    ROSALYN
After all this time, you're due.

Rosalyn does a last minute check of her makeup in the
mirror.

                    ROSALYN (Cont'd)
I just pray you aren't
disappointed again.

                    ALICE
Me, too.

                    ROSALYN
Well, you never know what's going
to happen, do you?

                    ALICE
No, you never know.

Rosalyn casually looks over the competition.

                    ROSALYN
Oh, Alice. Your shoe. You've got
a piece of toilet paper stuck to
it. Attention to detail. An
important trait for a partner.

                    ALICE
Thanks for the tip.

Rosalyn turns to go as Alice removes the toilet paper
from her shoe. Then Alice looks up and SEES that
Rosalyn has got the hem of her skirt and a toilet seat
protector accidentally tucked into the back of her panty
hose.

                    ALICE
          Oh, Roz, your--

                    ROSALYN
          Attention to detail. That's what
          separates the good from the great.

                    ALICE
          Thanks, Roz. I'll remember that.

INT. R.J.'S OFFICE - DAY

R.J. is signing a number of papers that his SECRETARY
puts under his pen, then whisks away. He's an Armani
suited man in his fifties, all smiles, in control.

Alice steps into the open doorway of the office. She's
nervous with anticipation.

                    ALICE
          You wanted to see me, R.J.?

                    R.J.
          Come on in, take a seat. I'll be
          with you in a moment.
               (to secretary)
          And get a standard partnership
          form ready for me, will you?

                    SECRETARY
          Yes, sir.

She gathers up the papers and walks by Alice on the way
out. There's a look of pity on her face. Uh oh. She
closes the door on the way out, and Alice sits down.

                    R.J.
          Alice, you know we plan to appoint
          a new partner today.

She straightens up a little, ready for the good news.

                    ALICE
          I'm sure you won't be disappointed
          in your choice, R.J.

                    R.J.
        We thought long and hard about
        this, Alice. In the end I think
        we've come up with the best woman
        for the job. We all have
        tremendous respect for you.

                    ALICE
        Thank you, R.J. I appreciate--

                    R.J.
        --which is why we're telling you
        first about Rosalyn Eckert's
        appointment.

The air whooshes out of Alice's lungs.

                    R.J. (Cont'd)
        Now I know you must be upset about
        not making partner, and I'm sorry.

Alice takes a beat to pull herself together.

                    ALICE
        Thanks, R.J. I'll take your "I'm
        sorry" to the market and see how
        many bags of groceries I can get
        for it.

                    R.J.
        It was really close, Alice. Down
        to the wire. We had a tough time
        deciding. It could have gone
        either way.

                    ALICE
        So why didn't it go my way? I'm
        just as competent and hard working
        as she is, and you know it.

                    R.J.
        It's just that Roz has more
        energy.

                    ALICE
        What you mean is, she's younger.

                    R.J.
        I didn't say that.

Alice stands up, towering over the seated R.J.

                    ALICE
        That's what you mean, isn't it?

                       R.J.
No, what I mean is, she's
available twenty-four hours a day
in the service of the firm. And
you're not.

                    ALICE
I have a daughter to take care of
and--

                    R.J.
--and she doesn't. That's my
point. The firm always comes
first for Roz. In the end that
was the difference.

                    ALICE
       (composing herself)
Is that all?

                    R.J.
Alice, the door is still open for
you. But if you want to make
partner, you'll have to try
harder.

Alice turns to go. She opens the door and finds
Rosalyn standing there.

                    ALICE
    Roz.

                  ROSALYN
    Alice.

Alice eyes her as she passes. SHE SEES that the toilet
protector and skirt are still tucked up into Roz's
panty hose.

                    ALICE
       (indicating Roz's
       backside)
Oh, I see you're wearing the new
partner's uniform. Attention to
detail, Roz. Makes all the
difference.

Rosalyn reaches around, feels the protector, and looks
mortified.

A sly smile crosses Alice's face and we

                              CUT TO:

Each of these drafts went through a series of print-outs and corrections before I would call it a draft. There was another "producers' draft" before we finally submitted it to Rysher. Unfortunately, Rysher went out of the movie business shortly thereafter and never made the film. It happens more often than you think. Fewer than one in twenty scripts bought by the studios makes it to the screen.

Photo Credits

Thelma & Louise, written by Callie Khouri, directed by Ridley Scott, MGM, page 3.

In & Out, written by Paul Rudnick, directed by Frank Oz, Paramount, page 5.

The Patriot, written by Robert Rodat, directed by Roland Emmerich, Columbia, page 21.

Erin Brockovich, written by Susannah Grant, directed by Steven Soderburgh, Jersey Films, page 28.

The Cable Guy, written by Lou Holtz, directed by Ben Stiller, Columbia, page 35.

Die Hard, screenplay by Jeb Stuart, based on the novel by Roderick Thorp, directed by John McTiernan, Fox, page 42.

Shakespeare in Love, written by Marc Norman and Tom Stoppard, directed by John Madden, Bedford Falls and Miramax, page 46.

Thelma & Louise, written by Callie Khouri, directed by Ridley Scott, MGM, page 53.

The Wizard of Oz, screenplay by Noel Langely, Forence Ryserson, and Edgar Allen Woolf, based on the book by L. Frank Baum, directed by Victor Fleming, MGM, page 63.

Kiss Kiss Bang Bang, screenplay by Shane Black, based on the novel by Brett Halliday, directed by Shane Black, Warner Brothers, page 100.

BIBLIOGRAPHY

Ackerman, Hal. *Write Screenplays that Sell: The Ackerman Way.* Los Angeles: Tallfellow Press, 2003.

Bowles, Stephen E., Mangravite, Ronald, and Zorn, Peter. *The Complete Screenwriter's Manual: A Comprehensive Reference of Format and Style.* Boston: Pearson, 2006.

Egri, Lajos. *The Art of Dramatic Writing.* New York: Touchstone, 1972.

Field, Syd. *Screenplay.* New York: Dell, 1994.

Gelfand, Janna E. *A Practical Guide to Flawless Screenplay Form.* Los Angeles: Get It Right Press, 2000.

Goldman, William. *Adventures in the Screen Trade.* New York: Warner Books, 1989.

Hunter, Lew. *Lew Hunter's Screenwriting 434.* New York: Penguin, 1993.

Hutzler, Laurie. *One Hour Screenwriter.* Santa Monica, CA: Emotional Toolbox, 2006.

Hutzler, Laurie. *The Character Map.* Santa Monica, CA: Emotional Toolbox.

Lerch, Jennifer. *500 Ways to Beat the Hollywood Script Reader.* New York: Simon and Schuster, 1999.

Riley, Christopher. *The Hollywood Standard. The Complete & Authoritative Guide to Script Format and Style.* Los Angeles: Michael Wiese Productions, 2005.

Seger, Linda. *Making a Good Script Great.* New York: Samuel French, 1994.

Strunk, William, Jr., and E. B. White. *The Elements of Style.* 4th edition. Boston: Allyn & Bacon/Longman Publishers, 1999.

Vogler, Christopher. *The Writer's Journey.* 3rd edition. Los Angeles: Michael Wiese Productions, 2007.

Walter, Richard. *Screenwriting. The Art, Craft and Business of Film and Television Writing.* New York: Plume, 1988.

Yoneda, Kathie Fong. *The Script Selling Game: A Hollywood Insider's Look at Getting Your Script Sold and Produced.* Los Angeles: Michael Wiese Productions, 2002.

And any screenplay you can get your hands on.

INDEX

About the Author

Paul Chitlik's writer/producer credits include *The New Twilight Zone*, *Who's the Boss*, *Brothers*, *Amen*, *Perfect Strangers*, *Small Wonder*, *Los Beltrán*, *V.I.P.*, *American Playhouse*, and the made-for-television movie *Alien Abduction* for UPN. He produced and directed numerous episodes of *US Customs Classified* and *Real Stories of the Highway Patrol*. Mr. Chitlik has created several pilots as well as written feature films for Rysher, NuImage, Mainline Releasing, and Promark. He has been nominated for a WGA Award and a GLAAD Media Award and has won a Genesis Award.

Chitlik also teaches screenwriting at UCLA, Loyola Marymount University, and ESCAC, the film school of the University of Barcelona, Spain.

He lives in Burbank, California.

Chitlik can be contacted at *therewritementor@yahoo.com*.

SAVE THE CAT!™ GOES TO THE MOVIES

THE SCREENWRITER'S GUIDE TO EVERY STORY EVER TOLD

BLAKE SNYDER

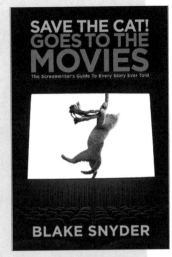

In the long-awaited sequel to his surprise bestseller, *Save the Cat!*, author and screenwriter Blake Snyder returns to form in a fast-paced follow-up that proves why his is the most talked-about approach to screenwriting in years. In the perfect companion piece to his first book, Snyder delivers even more insider's information gleaned from a 20-year track record as "one of Hollywood's most successful spec screenwriters," giving you the clues to write *your* movie.

Designed for screenwriters, novelists, and movie fans, this book gives readers the key breakdowns of the 50 most instructional movies from the past 30 years. From *M*A*S*H* to *Crash*, from *Alien* to *Saw*, from *10* to *Eternal Sunshine of the Spotless Mind*, Snyder reveals how screenwriters who came before you tackled the same challenges you are facing with the film you want to write — or the one you are currently working on.

Writing a "rom-com"? Check out the "Buddy Love" chapter for a "beat for beat" dissection of *When Harry Met Sally...* plus references to 10 other great romantic comedies that will make your story sing.

Want to execute a great mystery? Go to the "Whydunit" section and learn about the "dark turn" that's essential to the heroes of *All the President's Men*, *Blade Runner*, *Fargo* and hip noir *Brick* — and see why ALL good stories, whether a Hollywood blockbuster or a Sundance award winner, follow the same rules of structure outlined in Snyder's breakthrough method.

If you want to sell your script and create a movie that pleases most audiences most of the time, the odds increase if you reference Snyder's checklists and see what makes 50 films tick. After all, both executives and audiences respond to the same elements good writers seek to master. They want to know the type of story they signed on for, and whether it's structured in a way that satisfies everyone. It's what they're looking for. And now, it's what you can deliver.

BLAKE SNYDER, besides selling million-dollar scripts to both Disney and Spielberg, is still "one of Hollywood's most successful spec screenwriters," having made another spec sale in 2006. An in-demand scriptcoach and seminar and workshop leader, Snyder provides information for writers through his website, *www.blakesnyder.com.*

$24.95 · 270 PAGES · ORDER NUMBER 75RLS · ISBN: 1932907351

THE WRITER'S JOURNEY
3RD EDITION

MYTHIC STRUCTURE FOR WRITERS

CHRISTOPHER VOGLER

BEST SELLER
OVER 170,000 COPIES SOLD!

See why this book has become an international best seller and a true classic. *The Writer's Journey* explores the powerful relationship between mythology and storytelling in a clear, concise style that's made it required reading for movie executives, screenwriters, playwrights, scholars, and fans of pop culture all over the world.

Both fiction and nonfiction writers will discover a set of useful myth-inspired storytelling paradigms (i.e., "The Hero's Journey") and step-by-step guidelines to plot and character development. Based on the work of Joseph Campbell, *The Writer's Journey* is a must for all writers interested in further developing their craft.

The updated and revised third edition provides new insights and observations from Vogler's ongoing work on mythology's influence on stories, movies, and man himself.

"This book is like having the smartest person in the story meeting come home with you and whisper what to do in your ear as you write a screenplay. Insight for insight, step for step, Chris Vogler takes us through the process of connecting theme to story and making a script come alive."
> – Lynda Obst, Producer, *Sleepless in Seattle, How to Lose a Guy in 10 Days;*
> Author, *Hello, He Lied*

"This is a book about the stories we write, and perhaps more importantly, the stories we live. It is the most influential work I have yet encountered on the art, nature, and the very purpose of storytelling."
> – Bruce Joel Rubin, Screenwriter, *Stuart Little 2, Deep Impact,*
> *Ghost, Jacob's Ladder*

CHRISTOPHER VOGLER is a veteran story consultant for major Hollywood film companies and a respected teacher of filmmakers and writers around the globe. He has influenced the stories of movies from *The Lion King* to *Fight Club* to *The Thin Red Line* and most recently wrote the first installment of *Ravenskull*, a Japanese-style manga or graphic novel. He is the executive producer of the feature film *P.S. Your Cat is Dead* and writer of the animated feature *Jester Till*.

$26.95 · 400 PAGES · ORDER NUMBER 76RLS · ISBN: 193290736x

THE MYTH OF MWP

In a dark time, a light bringer came along, leading the curious and the frustrated to clarity and empowerment. It took the well-guarded secrets out of the hands of the few and made them available to all. It spread a spirit of openness and creative freedom, and built a storehouse of knowledge dedicated to the betterment of the arts.

The essence of the Michael Wiese Productions (MWP) is empowering people who have the burning desire to express themselves creatively. We help them realize their dreams by putting the tools in their hands. We demystify the sometimes secretive worlds of screenwriting, directing, acting, producing, film financing, and other media crafts.

By doing so, we hope to bring forth a realization of 'conscious media' which we define as being positively charged, emphasizing hope and affirming positive values like trust, cooperation, self-empowerment, freedom, and love. Grounded in the deep roots of myth, it aims to be healing both for those who make the art and those who encounter it. It hopes to be transformative for people, opening doors to new possibilities and pulling back veils to reveal hidden worlds.

MWP has built a storehouse of knowledge unequaled in the world, for no other publisher has so many titles on the media arts. Please visit www.mwp.com where you will find many free resources and a 25% discount on our books. Sign up and become part of the wider creative community!

Onward and upward,

Michael Wiese
Publisher/Filmmaker

FILM & VIDEO BOOKS

SCREENWRITING | WRITING

And the Best Screenplay Goes to... | Dr. Linda Seger | $26.95
Archetypes for Writers | Jennifer Van Bergen | $22.95
Bali Brothers | Lacy Waltzman, Matthew Bishop, Michael Wiese | $12.95
Cinematic Storytelling | Jennifer Van Sijll | $24.95
Could It Be a Movie? | Christina Hamlett | $26.95
Creating Characters | Marisa D'Vari | $26.95
Crime Writer's Reference Guide, The | Martin Roth | $20.95
Deep Cinema | Mary Trainor-Brigham | $19.95
Elephant Bucks | Sheldon Bull | $24.95
Fast, Cheap & Written That Way | John Gaspard | $26.95
Hollywood Standard – 2nd Edition, The | Christopher Riley | $18.95
Horror Screenwriting | Devin Watson | $24.95
I Could've Written a Better Movie than That! | Derek Rydall | $26.95
Inner Drives | Pamela Jaye Smith | $26.95
Moral Premise, The | Stanley D. Williams, Ph.D. | $24.95
Myth and the Movies | Stuart Voytilla | $26.95
Power of the Dark Side, The | Pamela Jaye Smith | $22.95
Psychology for Screenwriters | William Indick, Ph.D. | $26.95
Reflections of the Shadow | Jeffrey Hirschberg | $26.95
Rewrite | Paul Chitlik | $16.95
Romancing the A-List | Christopher Keane | $18.95
Save the Cat! | Blake Snyder | $19.95
Save the Cat! Goes to the Movies | Blake Snyder | $24.95
Screenwriting 101 | Neill D. Hicks | $16.95
Screenwriting for Teens | Christina Hamlett | $18.95
Script-Selling Game, The | Kathie Fong Yoneda | $16.95
Stealing Fire From the Gods, 2nd Edition | James Bonnet | $26.95
Talk the Talk | Penny Penniston | $24.95
Way of Story, The | Catherine Ann Jones | $22.95
What Are You Laughing At? | Brad Schreiber | $19.95
Writer's Journey – 3rd Edition, The | Christopher Vogler | $26.95
Writer's Partner, The | Martin Roth | $24.95
Writing the Action Adventure Film | Neill D. Hicks | $14.95
Writing the Comedy Film | Stuart Voytilla & Scott Petri | $14.95
Writing the Killer Treatment | Michael Halperin | $14.95
Writing the Second Act | Michael Halperin | $19.95
Writing the Thriller Film | Neill D. Hicks | $14.95
Writing the TV Drama Series, 2nd Edition | Pamela Douglas | $26.95
Your Screenplay Sucks! | William M. Akers | $19.95

FILMMAKING

Film School | Richard D. Pepperman | $24.95
Power of Film, The | Howard Suber | $27.95

PITCHING

Perfect Pitch – 2nd Edition, The | Ken Rotcop | $19.95
Selling Your Story in 60 Seconds | Michael Hauge | $12.95

SHORTS

Filmmaking for Teens, 2nd Edition | Troy Lanier & Clay Nichols | $24.95
Making It Big in Shorts | Kim Adelman | $22.95

BUDGET | PRODUCTION MANAGEMENT

Film & Video Budgets, 5th Updated Edition | Deke Simon | $26.95
Film Production Management 101 | Deborah S. Patz | $39.95

DIRECTING | VISUALIZATION

Animation Unleashed | Ellen Besen | $26.95

Cinematography for Directors | Jacqueline Frost | $29.95
Citizen Kane Crash Course in Cinematography | David Worth | $19.95
Directing Actors | Judith Weston | $26.95
Directing Feature Films | Mark Travis | $26.95
Fast, Cheap & Under Control | John Gaspard | $26.95
Film Directing: Cinematic Motion, 2nd Edition | Steven D. Katz | $27.95
Film Directing: Shot by Shot | Steven D. Katz | $27.95
Film Director's Intuition, The | Judith Weston | $26.95
First Time Director | Gil Bettman | $27.95
From Word to Image, 2nd Edition | Marcie Begleiter | $26.95
I'll Be in My Trailer! | John Badham & Craig Modderno | $26.95
Master Shots | Christopher Kenworthy | $24.95
Setting Up Your Scenes | Richard D. Pepperman | $24.95
Setting Up Your Shots, 2nd Edition | Jeremy Vineyard | $22.95
Working Director, The | Charles Wilkinson | $22.95

DIGITAL | DOCUMENTARY | SPECIAL

Digital Filmmaking 101, 2nd Edition | Dale Newton & John Gaspard | $26.95
Digital Moviemaking 3.0 | Scott Billups | $24.95
Digital Video Secrets | Tony Levelle | $26.95
Greenscreen Made Easy | Jeremy Hanke & Michele Yamazaki | $19.95
Producing with Passion | Dorothy Fadiman & Tony Levelle | $22.95
Special Effects | Michael Slone | $31.95

EDITING

Cut by Cut | Gael Chandler | $35.95
Cut to the Chase | Bobbie O'Steen | $24.95
Eye is Quicker, The | Richard D. Pepperman | $27.95
Film Editing | Gael Chandler | $34.95
Invisible Cut, The | Bobbie O'Steen | $28.95

SOUND | DVD | CAREER

Complete DVD Book, The | Chris Gore & Paul J. Salamoff | $26.95
Costume Design 101, 2nd Edition | Richard La Motte | $24.95
Hitting Your Mark, 2nd Edition | Steve Carlson | $22.95
Sound Design | David Sonnenschein | $19.95
Sound Effects Bible, The | Ric Viers | $26.95
Storyboarding 101 | James Fraioli | $19.95
There's No Business Like Soul Business | Derek Rydall | $22.95
You Can Act! | D. W. Brown | $24.95

FINANCE | MARKETING | FUNDING

Art of Film Funding, The | Carole Lee Dean | $26.95
Bankroll | Tom Malloy | $26.95
Complete Independent Movie Marketing Handbook, The | Mark Steven Bosko | $39.95
Getting the Money | Jeremy Jusso | $26.95
Independent Film and Videomakers Guide – 2nd Edition, The | Michael Wiese | $29.95
Independent Film Distribution | Phil Hall | $26.95
Shaking the Money Tree, 3rd Edition | Morrie Warshawski | $26.95

MEDITATION | ART

Mandalas of Bali | Dewa Nyoman Batuan | $39.95

OUR FILMS

Dolphin Adventures: DVD | Michael Wiese and Hardy Jones | $24.95
Hardware Wars: DVD | Written and Directed by Ernie Fosselius | $14.95
On the Edge of a Dream | Michael Wiese | $16.95
Sacred Sites of the Dalai Lamas– DVD, The | Documentary by Michael Wiese | $24.95